THE TRANSCENDENT SELF

BOOKS BY THE AUTHOR

A Light to the Gentiles
Religion and Personality
Personality Fulfillment in the Spiritual Life
Existential Foundations of Psychology
The Art of Existential Counseling
The Demon and the Dove (co-author)
Personality Fulfillment in the Religious Life
The Vowed Life
The Emergent Self (co-author)
The Participant Self (co-author)
On Being Involved
Living Creatively
On Being Yourself
Spirituality and the Gentle Life
In Search of Spiritual Identity
Dynamics of Spiritual Self Direction
Tell Me Who I Am (co-author)
The Woman at the Well
Looking for Jesus
Am I Living a Spiritual Life? (co-author)
The Transcendent Self

THE TRANSCENDENT SELF

Formative Spirituality of the Middle, Early, and Later Years of Life

By

ADRIAN VAN KAAM, C.S.Sp.

DIMENSION BOOKS, INC.
Denville, New Jersey 07834

Published by Dimension Books, Inc.

Denville, New Jersey 07834

Library of Congress Catalog Card No. 79-54044
ISBN 087193-074-9

Imprimi Potest: *Rev. Philip J. Haggerty, C.S.Sp.*
Provincial

Nihil Obstat: *Rev. William J. Winter, S.T.D.*
Censor Librorum

Imprimatur: *Most Rev. Vincent M. Leonard, D.D.*
Bishop of Pittsburgh

June 22, 1979

TABLE OF CONTENTS

PREFACE

Transcendence is one of the fundamental dynamics of human and spiritual formation. Each person approaches his or her full potential by way of transitions from lower to higher forms of spiritual life. Transcendence crises often accompany these transitions. They can take place at any moment of our spiritual formation, provided they are not repressed. They can be delayed, fostered or precipitated. Unsettling experiences, for example, can precipitate crises that might otherwise have emerged later in life. Good novitiates and formation institutes may evoke crises of transition in those who do not flee from the opportunities for transformation provided for them in these and like settings.

When the climate for formation is favorable in a culture, crises of transition begin earlier in life, are less striking, and succeed one another gradually and smoothly. Such gradual succession is unlikely in cultures that neglect spiritual formation. Many people in these cultures share a less transcendent outlook on life. During the first half of life, they leave little time or space for spiritual reflection. In mid-life, however, a number of them are forced to acknowl-

edge the limits of their vital and functional possibilities. Because of the earlier denial of such limits,
the mid-life crisis of transition may find them unpre-
pared. Striking psychological problems may result
from this breakthrough of a first experience of
finitude and contingency.

The resulting panic in a number of people made the
transcendence crisis — for the first time in history —
also an object of study for sciences other than
formative spirituality. Anthropologists, medical
researchers, psychologists, sociologists, and other
specialists added their insights to those of the age-old
wisdom of formative spirituality. They would usually
refer to this transcendence crisis as the mid-life crisis.

Clearly, the mid-life crisis can highlight certain
aspects of any formation crisis. Formative spirituality
considers this crisis in light of its own more universal
concerns and categories. It links its considerations as
always to the every day formation experiences of
people, while taking into account the findings of the
incarnational sciences, mentioned above, and the
insights of such directive sciences as theology and
philosophy. Their contributions have to be translated
and integrated into the basic categories of a foundational formative spirituality developed in part in
this book.

The mid-life crisis is a paradigm of all transcendence crises; it demonstrates the dynamics of
transcendence in formation as a whole. This book
brings the reader into dialogue with his or her own
every day experience as the basis of the transcend-

ence crisis and its possibilities for transformation. Practical suggestions may help each reader to deal effectively with these crisis moments in his or her own life and that of others. Because of this practical intent, scientific reports, while utilized extensively in the research are purposefully kept in the background so that they do not interfere with the experimental dialogue into which the reader is initiated as an aid to his personal formation and transformation in Christ.

This book is meant for people in all walks of life and of all ages who want to grow in self-insight and true self-unfolding or who are called upon to assist others in their spiritual self-formation.

It is the author's pleasant duty to express his gratefulness to the Executive Director of the graduate Institute of Formative Spirituality at Duquesne, Dr. Susan Annette Muto, who suggested many improvements in style and content. Appreciation is due also to Rev. Thaddeus Maida, S.T.L., and Mrs. John Otis Carney, who read parts of the manuscript and helped, by their comments, to enhance its readability. Finally, Mrs. Tina Whitehead deserves acknowledgment for her patient typing and retyping of the drafts of this book.

Adrian van Kaam, C.S.Sp.
Institute of Formative Spirituality
Duquesne University
June, 1979

CHAPTER I
THE TRANSCENDENT SELF AND THE MID-LIFE CRISIS

The mid-life crisis is a popular theme of talk shows, books, pamphlets and articles. Our fascination with it is more than a fad; it points to the fact that an increasing number of people face a transcendence crisis in the second half of life. Changes in themselves and in their life situation challenge them to go beyond or "transcend" their familiar attitudes or customary ways. The upheaval we witness in the world today and in our churches seems to complicate their mid-life problems. So does the fact that fewer people passed through earlier minor crises of transcendence that would have made the mid-life one less noticeable. Others again experience the crisis later in life or not at all.

The crisis sets in for many of us when our vital powers and functional effectiveness are declining. We suspect that our life has to take on a deeper form which transcends our past outlook and attitudes.

Working through the spiritual problems of middle-aging is not a privilege for those who dabble in psychology. It is not a luxury for those partial to introspection but a necessity for all of us, especially if we neglected the gradual cultivation of a more transcendent view of reality. The mid-life crisis is ultimately a spiritual one that challenges us to transcend a mainly vitalistic or functional appraisal of life. Its solution involves more than a psychological compromise or a program of physical exercise. New hobbies and entertainments can be part of the solution, but they are not the whole story.

The mid-life crisis implies as well an awareness of our mortality and finitude. This happens because we begin to experience our human confinement in a way we can no longer deny; we do not feel as fit, as clever or as effective as we used to. Even those not much given to reflection on the meaning of their lives are forced now to search for a deeper reason to go on. That reason is found in a region of our personality where many of us do not feel much at home, for we must turn inwardly to the transcendent dimension of our spiritual life.

The mid-life crisis is an invitation to become more aware of that dimension. The lessening of our vital powers and functional effectiveness opens us to the possibility of a more inward, peaceful style of living, one that is richer and more rewarding than anything we felt before. If we begin to understand our mid-age problems in this manner, we may experience the crisis both as a gift and as an opportunity to make up for the minor transcendence crises we may have ignored in the past.

The mid-life crisis is marked not only by a diminishment of power and mastery but also by a threat to our familiar form of life. Our youth-oriented culture does not prepare us for this shift. The underestimation of old people and the focus on youth suggests a dead end for middle age. This treatment can be terrifying. We begin to fear a kind of formlessness in middle-age. As an antidote we may cling anxiously to our prior form of life via a frenzied outburst of activity. However, there is another alternative. We can begin the long search for a self-formation that opens us to unexplored avenues of growth.

The mid-life crisis is a crisis of transcendence; its solution is, therefore, a spiritual one. For many of us this solution is bound to the wisdom of established religious traditions. Others find a transcendent way not directly linked with the teachings of organized religions.

In this book we are interested in a transcendent solution inspired by Christian spirituality. This view immediately raises the question: Is there a difference between the natural and the supernatural solution? What is the connection between the two? Do they influence one another or are they more or less independent?

Some may think that the spiritual life of the Christian, its problems, crises and solutions, is only a question of grace. In that case the transcendent solution of this crisis would be dependent on God only. We pray, surrender to Him and wait for the solution to come from Him, ready-made, as it were.

It is true that the solution of this crisis is a grace of God. His grace, however, does not work in us without our cooperation. Usually God attunes the grace of a transcendent solution to the problem-solving ability He has given us. Grace does not change our problems miraculously like Jesus changed water into wine. The solution is the result of a human struggle sustained and enlightened by grace. It is a struggle for new insight, for detachment from former directives and forms of life — a struggle that encompasses all we know about this crisis, its symptoms and meanings, as well as its opportunity for growth. To see such insights as providential conditions for a Christian solution of the transcendence crisis is to withdraw nothing from the dominion of grace. Rather every aspect of the crisis is subsumed under the mystery of divine generosity.

The mid-life crisis is like the winter season of our life. As we move into winter, it is obvious that nature has changed. Autumn has stripped the trees and their colorful foliage is a thing of the past. This change of seasons is an integral part of nature's year. Although we often wish to hasten the dismal days toward spring, we realize that one season is needed to bring about the other. So we wait patiently.

Human nature affords us the same possibility of changing seasons that seem to be interwoven in our life story of transcendent unfolding. In the "summers" of life, we experience exhilaration, openness, the freedom to challenge and be challenged. In "autumns" we suffer a loss or stripping of vitality. In the "springs" we know the wholeness and growth of peace and joy. Before this time of newness and growth, there was "winter" — a period of defeat, or a time of struggle and suffering.

To most of us, winter seems bleak and dead while in actuality growth is taking place in hiddenness, below the soil. During the winter months, plant life withdraws to recoup its forces and to prepare for the new thrust of spring.

With adequate reflection, we may see the same rhythm of nature exemplified in our own lives. There are phases throughout life when we must withdraw into our inner center and let the darkness come upon us. During middle age, life seems for a number of us to lose its meaning. Obligations become oppressive. At this time weariness often takes over.

As we do not see what is happening below the surface during nature's winter months, so in faith we must believe that although He is presently unseen, God is affecting an interior growth in us. Being at home with this mystery may help us to wait patiently while seeking a way through the darkness.

If we believe that this darkness is allowed by God in love, we may find that He is calling us to a deeper interiority: to shed the darkness of what we feel for the light of who we are.

In our solitude we may discover that we are extinguishing the light ourselves by an overly functional life, by "doing" in preference to "being," by interior noise rather than quiet. If we honestly evaluate ourselves in this season of our life, we may see that the darkness is in reality a light to see what must be changed. Then in God's time He may once again bring forth within us a new spring and a realization that

> . . . *winter is past,*
> *the rains are over and gone.*
> *The flowers appear on the earth.*
> *The season of glad songs has come,*
> *the cooing of the turtledove is heard*
> *in our land.*   (Sg. 2:11-12)

Chapter II

THE MIDDLE YEARS:
FUNCTIONAL PHASE AND FORMATION

To understand the crisis of transcendence that manifests itself in a number of people in mid-life, we have to understand mid-life itself. The middle years begin approximately at the age of 30. For many people, though by no means for all, they embrace two phases of self-formation. The first phase is marked by the heightened formation of the functional dimension of their spiritual life. The second phase complements the former by an emphasis on the formation of the transcendent aspect of their spirituality.

It would be impossible to assign exact time limits for each of these periods. We may say roughly that for certain persons the first phase reaches its height between 30 and 44; the period of transcendence happens for them between 44 and 55. For others these formations may take place earlier or later in life, or occur so gradually that they are almost unnoticeable.

Between these two phases there is for many a turning point, a shifting from one phase to the other. Because the shift can be considerable, it may be accompanied by a crisis. This is often called the mid-life crisis; it falls somewhere in the beginning of the second phase of the middle years. If this crisis happens, it is an exemplary case of the many crises of spiritual transcendence that may happen at any time of life.

Functional Phase of Mid-Life

Our spiritual selfhood emerges in many phases. These foster the formation of different dimensions of our spirituality. We call them, therefore, the temporal dimensions of the spiritual life. Infancy, childhood, adolescence, young adulthood, the functional and transcendent mid-years and old age are all examples of such temporal dimensions. Each of them can give rise to the formation of one or the other special aspect of our spirituality.

The first phase of the mid-years falls for many between the beginning of the 30's and the 40's. Their functioning seems to reach its highest effectiveness during that period. They may attain the fullness of their performance potential around the end of this phase, between 40 and 44.

The temporal self-dimension these people usually experienced before this period of the 30's was that of "young adulthood." As young adults in their later 20's they became integrated into society. During that period many committed themselves to a vocational and occupational life form. They chose their life partner or the single life and decided what they were going to do. They settled down in their commitments. In their late 20's they felt at home in life while feeling that the best was yet to come. "Real life" they imagined as still stretching before them. The approaching period of the 30's seemed to them an opportunity to make their mark and to find their most effective self-expression in society.

If we belong to this group of people, we may enter in our 30's the functional phase of mid-life, which for many begins after this period of young adulthood. To be successful in this phase is to enjoy the experience of our expanding skillfulness. We feel the power of our ambitions, the effectiveness of our actions. These ambitions are not necessarily self-centered. They may be noble ambitions to serve community and society. We want to incarnate our dreams and ideals in our families and careers. We feel inspired to create order in our lives and surroundings. When we meet resistance, we feel vital and skillful enough to cope with it as well as we can.

How well this period of the 30's works for us depends on how well we passed through earlier periods of self-emergence. Our growth during former phases of emergence may have been stunted. We may have ignored grace opportunities for formative transcendence crises. Perhaps we neglected some of the formative assignments each phase imposed on us or failed the test of one of these temporal dimensions. This means that our spiritual self is underdeveloped, not fully ready for optimal unfolding in this stage. We have first to make up for this neglect or failure. If the back log of unfinished formative assignments is considerable, some spiritual direction may be advisable. Such direction may have to be sustained by therapeutic counseling or psychotherapy.

To be successful in the 30's, our environment too has to be favorable. It must provide us with opportunities to implement our projects, to try out our skills, and to realize in some measure our ambitions. If not, we may feel overcome by resentment and frustration, leading in turn to despair, aggression or rebellion. In extreme cases suicidal tendencies may be aroused. When we cannot live out our reasonable ambitions, we may become victims of fringe groups that promise their followers satisfaction of their ambitions and an outlet for their anger and frustrations.

This period of the 30's enables many people to develop more of their sensate, manual and experimental skills. They develop them in coping with the practical demands of their jobs, families and communities.

The kind of intellect preferred by many in their 30's is critical, pragmatic reason. The intuitive, contemplative intellect comes into play far less than it is likely to in the second phase of mid-life. Something similar can be said of their will. The most radical kind of willing is our loving openness to the Transcendent and to world, society and others in light of the Transcendent. In this openness we may experience simple aspirations and inspirations. We may subsequently try to implement these on the practical level of everyday tasks to be done, promises to be kept, commitments to be realized.

Our will, insofar as it wills this concrete execution, is the *executive will.* Another kind of willing or of loving openness to that which transcends and sustains practical execution is the *transcendent will.* The phase of the 30's mainly strengthens the executive will while the phase after the turning point usually gives the transcendent will more room for unfolding.

Each dimension of our emerging life form derives its dynamism from the strivings typical of that dimension. Strivings that prevail on the functional level are designated *ambitions.* We experience in this phase a heightening of our ambitions for practical achievement and the pursuit of excellence.

It stands to reason that we feel good and vitally alive during these years if we are able to perform effectively. Success presupposes, however, that we have some real abilities; that we keep our ambitions within the limits of these abilities; that our past life not saddle us with too many problems and unresolved conflicts; and that our environment offer us opportunities for living out our reasonable ambitions at least in some measure. If these conditions are fulfilled and our vital strength is normal for this period, many of us may experience the highest functional confidence and assertiveness we shall ever know. It is also true that the more self-assertive, secure and successful we are at this stage, the more we are tempted to neglect the cultivation of a transcendent view of life; in that case we may be more severely disturbed by the uncertainty and loss of power we shall experience later in the mid-life crisis.

Advantages and Disadvantages
of the Functional Phase

The mid-life crisis reminds us that the transcendent dimension is the source of our selfhood. Without it we would lose our human aspirations. We would be driven only by passion and vital desire or by self-centered ambitions. Therefore transcendent aspirations are already preconsciously at work during spiritual formation phases that do not predominantly focus on the unfolding of the transcendent dimension itself. The functional phase is thus not without transcendent influence. The same is true of the earlier vital phase of our spiritual unfolding.

Vital passion and functional ambition are gifts. They give flavor and vigor to our spiritual life; they enable us to incarnate our aspirations in society in effective and attractive ways. Yet it is crucial that our passions and ambitions remain open to the messages of our transcendent self.

During the functional period of mid-life, this openness remains for many only implicit. Practical achievement moves to the foreground of their attention; communion with the Transcendent remains in the background.

While our intention may be to perform well in service of humanity, there is always the danger of becoming so absorbed in achievement for its own sake that we lose contact with the Transcendent. It is normal that our activity in this period be primarily directed towards growth in skills; towards conquest and possession of the material world; towards poise and politically adroit interaction with society; towards mastery of the practical aspects of our home life, vocation, or career. We are planners and builders, organizers and technicians. There is nothing wrong with being that way as long as our ambitions are not totally closed off from transcendent motivations.

Being successful and gaining recognition are not wrong. What is harmful is excessive concern over achievement: we are never at ease; we are always worried about power, possession, status and success. "Isolated" functional ambition sees people and things only in terms of goals to be achieved, feats to be accomplished, a reputation to be made. Some of these aims are undoubtedly excellent. We should strive after them without compulsion. They may be in line with our divine destiny. However, achievements are at odds with the unique divine image at the core of our life if they have to be forced forward under constant tension and the keeping up of pretenses.

The congenial unfolding of the functional dimension of the spiritual life is gentle and gracious, without overexertion, undue speed and aggression. In this stage of the mid-life we may be tempted to prove something, to be someone, to set a record in terms of numbers, marks or name. We may labor under the erroneous conviction that a lack of force, impatience and willfulness will diminish our effectiveness. We rush to achieve things, to obtain what we want as quickly as possible, to collect "useful" acquaintances, practical information, honors, the "right" invitations and possessions.

The achievement-oriented person in his 30's becomes impatient with his limitations; he rejects himself as he is and drives himself beyond his abilities. He frets about failure. It is difficult for him to see that failure and success — each in its own way — are pointers toward his true life direction.

We should try always to relate our functional endeavors to our spiritual formation. During this stage our energies ought to be concentrated on expanding and stabilizing our careers, on buying and improving a house of our own; on gaining a certain status among family, peers and neighbors; on securing a sound future. The Christian in this phase should energetically build a solid substructure that will support him and his family after the mid-life turning point when he will be less effective in the expansion of his resources. What he has to be wary of is the expectation that the attainment of any or all of these projects will in and by itself fulfill him completely. Indispensable as they may be, they are not an assurance of fulfillment. To see them otherwise is to idolize them. The person in his 30's, who has lost touch with his spirit and its desire for the Infinite, may believe that such functional conditions are final aims. Because of this illusion he will be badly equipped to deal with the mid-life crisis later.

Briefly, the person must build a reasonable economic and social substructure, but he should not be enslaved to it. He must now allow his life to be absorbed by one thing only: economic gain and position.

Further Disadvantages of this Phase

Higher aspirations were more alive in the former period of young adulthood between 20 and 33. Now, preoccupation with establishing oneself firmly in a pragmatic society, the experience of unfairness and ruthlessness, the draining effect of constant competition, the numbing of the daily grind, the increasing workload — all may dim for certain people the ideals of early adulthood.

Another danger in the 30's concerns the kind of failure we cannot yet cope with. To bear with failure and suffering, we must see them against the horizon of transcendent meaning. Such meanings are more readily available to many of us after the mid-life crisis. But, because of a neglect of minor transcendence crises, we may not have developed as yet sufficient inner resources. We cannot come to terms with unexpected setbacks. A cynical or sarcastic mood of bitter resignation often replaces patient dialogue with the disappointments of this period.

Ambition can give rise to overachievement and hypertension. Toward the end of the 30's excessive self-exertion may result in exhaustion and the reactivation of slumbering neuroses. In his imagination the person may experience any failure as a total defeat. He feels as if life has lost its meaning. Unfortunately, the main meaning of life may be for him functional-social success. His appraisal of failure is not realistic. The devastating experience of defeat may be due also to previous overestimation of one's capacities. Buoyed by vitality and initial success, the person overrated his abilities; sadly for him others may have concurred in this misapprehension.

Another source of disappointment is excessive ambition. Our achievement culture compounds the difficulties that are already associated with the inclination of the 30's to unrealistic standards of performance. Such criteria may carry over in the realm of spiritual formation. They give rise there to perfectionism. Such perfectionism hinders relaxed openness to transcendent experience. The mid-life crisis is marked by the announcement of transcendent values that have been ignored for too long a time. The more steeped we are in functional perfectionism, the less receptive we can be to disclosures of transcendence.

Another danger of the 30's may be that not enough time and energy is left for the development of deeper human relationships. We may collect numerous acquaintances but neglect the cultivation of friendships in depth. The competitive atmosphere may limit the growth of such friendships among colleagues. Even at home the business orientation may lessen opportunities for intimate love encounter between the marriage partners and for long hours of play and involvement with the children. The loneliness of the mid-life crisis in some people will be accentuated by lack of love and friendship.

Briefly, the danger of this phase is that we can slide

into an exclusive concern with effectiveness, measurable success, status and position.

Further Advantages of this Phase

Are there any advantages to this phase besides those of an increase in skillfulness and the securing of our niche in society?

One of the great tasks that face us at this time is the strengthening of a self-reliant, effective ego. This ego-strength enables us to organize and maintain the conditions that facilitate ongoing spiritual formation. Ego-strength makes it possible to embody and defend our unique life direction in the midst of adverse situations; it allows us to work effectively for humanity; to stand up for peace and justice; to participate courageously in the adventure of history.

Without ego-strength we are easily blown in all kinds of directions with every wind of change. We may betray our own call in life, seduced by stronger egos who want to get us involved in their calling.

Some of us are called to commit our lives to the cause of social justice, woman's liberation, service to the third world, slum clearance, ecumenism, encounter movements, eastern mysticism, scholarship, art, and so on. But we should not be seduced or brainwashed into any such service. It should be a free decision based on an honest life call. The mid-life crisis may make some of us more vulnerable to the claim of fanatics who purport to know the exclusive way in which to make the remainder of our life meaningful: meaning *their* way. Only when our ego develops well in this first period of mid-life are we able to resist the tyranny of the foreign mission fanatic, the social justice fanatic, the scholarship fanatic, the mysticism fanatic, and like others. In the midst of our mid-life vulnerability, we should remain alert to the religious or social fanatic who tries to involve everyone exclusively in the enterprise he or she feels temperamentally at home in. We may be at their mercy if we fail to strengthen our ego during the phase of functional spiritual formation. In the second half of mid-life we may be victimized by religious or social lobbyists, prying into and playing on guilt feelings that are easily aroused at this time. We may lose our own unique life direction and risk courting deformation rather than formation.

The same ego-strength and self-discipline will enable us to incarnate concretely our unique life direction in all the dimensions of our personality. The critical ability, increased discipline and rationality, which are the gifts of this period, will grant us a powerful protection against any false and floating spirituality. Later, in the transcendent phase of the middle years delusive mysticism, religious sentimentality and illusion may tempt us. Even genuine mystical experience needs a strong ego to prevent an inundation of the psyche by floating, illusory feelings that can lead to a mental breakdown.

Problem of Critical Functioning and Appraisal

We mentioned the strong development of the rational, critical intellect in many people in their 30's.

During the later transcendent phase, it helps them to prevent the "floating spirituality" that ensues from religious experiences that are not wisely appraised. The rational intellect grounds these experiences in the wisdom of doctrine and tradition; it tests them against the demands of everyday reality and subjects them, if necessary, to other people wiser and more experienced in these matters.

This same down-to-earth rationality keeps us realistic and "level-headed" in our human and social endeavors. It is an essential part of an harmonious, effective spiritual life.

For all its advantages rationality can become counter-productive if developed excessively and onesidedly. This essential aspect should not become the whole of our spiritual life.

Our own language can give us a clue to a too exclusive dominance of critical rationality. Are we inclined to harsh statements? Are our judgments mellowed by gentleness and compassion? Are we overly critical? Does that lead sometimes to pessimism? Perhaps scepticism? Do we mainly see the failings of ourselves and others? Do we value things only on basis of their effectiveness? Do we become cynical? Is our main question always: How much can I make on it? What can I do with it practically? How does it solve problems? Are we inclined to deride symbolic or poetic thought? Is it for us a sign of regression, immaturity and naivete?

One advantage of the gift of critical appraisal is that it enables us to separate values from their "cultural packages." This is a necessary condition for growth in foundational spirituality. We become more sharply aware of our own and other's infidelity to the values we profess. This awareness inspires us to a revision of our values. We interiorized them blindly earlier in life, but now we may discover that they are not truly ours. We need gentle patience if such revision is to be formative and not destructive.

In the 30's — as well as in the 20's — patience may be lacking. Our reappraisal of values that direct our culture and lives is often made too fast. As a result we may break abruptly with the tradition in which we have been reared. We distance ourselves arrogantly from our family or community. Critical reason helps us to disclose false accretions of true values. Such deformations are always present in ourselves and in any human community. The danger is overreaction. We cut ourselves off not only from timebound accretions but from the sources of transcendent wisdom contained in traditions. Losing access to such sources makes it difficult for us to turn inward in a balanced way during the mid-life crisis. This crisis cannot be solved on basis of critical-rational analysis alone. The deeper formation it invites us to is only possible in formative interaction with the age-old wisdom of time-tested spiritual traditions.

Critical onesidedness tempts us to cut our ties prematurely. Upheavals in society or religion heighten this inclination. Any upheaval spawns a violent reappraisal of customs and values dear to former generations. It may encourage us to uproot ourselves from our spiritual ground. We commit cultural suicide. Not satisfied with purification, we strive for extirpation of our traditional values. Cut off from living tradition, we experience sooner or later that neither critical rationality nor personal and contemporary experience nourish a meaningful existence. Our life becomes a lost life.

A sad testimony to this loss of meaning is the "lost generations." They always appear after wars or social and religious transformations. These generations draw many of their adherents from the early mid-life period.

De-idolization

In the formation periods of childhood, adolescence and early adulthood, we are less faced with the demands of daily reality than in the functional phase of the 30's. The former periods gave rise to many ideals. These were formed more or less abstractly and imaginatively. There was a natural tendency to idolize certain people, institutions, positions and occupations. Now in the 30's these ideals are tested out in daily functioning and found to be wanting. The result is disenchantment with the ideals of the past. Practical confrontation with church and society may lead to disappointment too. The less realistic our life expectations, the greater the disillusion.

The fruit of disillusion can be "de-idolization." De-idolization does not deny the kernel of truth contained in former ideals. It purifies our ideals from exaltation; it liberates them from what is fallible and vulnerable.

Idealizing is due not only to our lack of contact with reality but also to our need for transcendence — a need which is always in search of an object. This explains our urge to idolize our ideals.

De-idolization is a formative task of the 30's. Such purification prepares us for a spiritual solution of an eventual transcendence crisis a number of people may experience during the second phase of the mid-years, in the late 40's and 50's. No one can attain transcendent experience who is still attached to idols.

Idolized ideals give rise to false spiritualities. They keep us away from the true Transcendent, who cannot be captured in any ideal or idol. Instead of binding us to the Transcendent, these ideals may tie some of us to idolized leaders. Fanaticism and hysteria follow. In their wake holy wars and violent destruction become a possibility. The massive self-destruction in Jonestown, Guyana, is a sombre reminder. These people, who desperately sought transcendent meaning in their lives, were fixated in an idealism that allowed them to be led by a fanatic idol. The combination of transcendent aspiration and spiritual immaturity blinded them to the self-preservative instincts of their vital life. They were duped in a suicidal pact to exclude the vital dimension of their spiritual life and thus led to a terrible death in the jungle.

For some persons in their 30's this disillusionment of ideals is too shocking to bear. In overreaction they do not quietly flow with the process of de-idolization but fall into the opposite extreme. What they idolized before they now demonize. They give up ideals and aspirations.

The aspiration for transcendent values that can give order and meaning to our endeavors is part of human nature. It can be refused and denied but not destroyed; the search for some transcendent meaning will express itself indirectly in disguised, distorted ways. For example, the functional person in his 30's, while demonizing all aspirations and ideals, may turn his functionality itself into a quasi-transcendent ideal. Realism then becomes functionalism or pragmatism. A fanatic devotion to what is practical, empirical, to what works, what brings results, dominates his life. He is marked by the zeal and defensiveness of the "true believer." He will derisively attack all "impractical nonsense," all truths that cannot be proven empirically. He becomes easily enslaved to psychologism, scientism, and technocracy as expressions of his quasi-spirituality.

Functionalism is fostered by the culture in which we are reared, for it idolizes the achieving person. This emphasis entails the danger that performance, status, success, consumption, and production become the exclusive directives of our formation. The quasi-spirituality of functional perfectionism is clearly a great temptation for successful people in their 30's.

Functional Phase and Relationships with Others

Prevalent in this period are progress and performance. Success is acknowledged by raises in salary, by promotion and public recognition. Progress implies passing others up on the ladder of reward; for many the period of the 30's is summed up by increasing competition.

Competition does not facilitate intimacy. When success is at stake, we are less inclined to solidarity. We may wish for comradeship but not at the expense of our own promotion. We may establish at most a negative solidarity based on shared defenses against perceived threats and dangers. Often such bonds of convenience show up in a shared critique of society and a common battle for improvement of labor and living conditions.

The relationships with family and friends also tend to be less intimate than in former or later phases of life. Too much time and attention seem to be absorbed by our pragmatic projects.

Sometimes there is a tension between certain adults in their 30's and adults in their 40's and 50's. A number of those in their 30's display aggressively their struggle for promotion; they pride themselves on their achievement ethos, on their vitality and cleverness in rational criticism. Such manifestations do not always endear them to adults who between 44 and 55 may experience an incipient decline of the same vitality and critical powers. They may respond to the achievement ethos of people in their 30's with a leadership ethos of their own. A number of them belittle the ambitiousness of early mid-life, pointing to lack of experience and wisdom. They demand the right to leadership positions. Their stand in turn evokes opposition. The struggle is intensified by the fact that a performance oriented society overrates the value of the functional phase.

How critical the 30's generation will be depends on the cultural situation. During or shortly after wars or cultural-religious upheavals, this generation tends to be more critical, disappointed and aggressive than usual. The tendency to criticism often marks them for a lifetime. Even when aging beyond this period, many maintain a lasting, latent readiness to protest.

The young who come along after a volatile wartime generation, or who follow a generation of social innovators as in the 60's, seem less aggressive in later life. They manifest a certain stability and contentment. The result of this change in attitude is a latent conflict between these later, more stable generations and those that preceded them. The revolutionaries of yesterday are now in advanced adulthood, but still marked by protest attitudes. In early mid-life they were the victims of social upheaval. That trauma may not completely leave them. Later generations find it difficult to empathize with super-annuated social or religious problems that still upset their predecessors. The former rebels in turn feel bitter that the glory of their past battles means so little to new generations.

Negative Feelings during the Early Mid-Years

When people look back later on this period of the 30's, they often mention that these years were not the happiest in their lives, even if they were among the most productive. When questioned many say that, on the contrary, the earlier years between 25 and 29 seem to have been the most pleasant for them. When single women are interviewed, many answer that the later years between 40 and 45 were their happiest.

What is it in the early mid-years that can give rise to unpleasant feelings? The period between 30 and 44 is one of increasing responsibility accompanied by the tensions that go with such new burdens. Combined with this, we face a decline in social mobility. This is experienced as becoming trapped in a small niche in history, becoming a social captive once and for all.

Interestingly enough, men at the end of young adulthood may experience a sudden increase in daydreams — a sign of rising expectations and expanding ambitions. After 33 daydreams disappear in many of them only to reappear again for those who experience the crisis of confinement in the later 40's. This reappearance may mean that transcendence begins dimly to announce itself with new possibilities of life or perhaps that the dreamer tries symbolically to recapture his waning vitality and ambitions. The decline in daydreaming during the functional phase in the 30's may signify a decline in spontaneity; playfulness is replaced by functional responsibility; it may mean a diminishment of joyfulness and exuberance.

Increasingly tied to occupation, family and children, many of us in the 30's sense that our life has taken on a more or less definite direction. Before this period life seemed more open, brimming with possibilities; directives were more tentative. Now we realize reluctantly that our opportunities and options are diminishing.

Youthful dreams have to be relinquished or cut to the prosaic size of daily reality. The demands of family, career, community make it impossible to live out to the full the grandiose designs of adolescence and early adulthood.

What has been learned academically, professionally and experientially has to be translated into practical deeds that are small, repetitious, and at times boring. Exciting projects become platitudes. What seemed glamorous in youthful speculation appears mundane when laid out in everyday routines. We no longer enjoy the unmixed blessing of fresh learning, of ever new encounters and adventurous travel. The tables are switched on us. Now we have to care about, to educate, and to take responsibility for a new generation and perhaps for a former generation too, when our parents become dependent on us. We feel a secret tinge of envy for the unencumbered youth still in his 20's.

Summary

The early mid-years of the 30's are the period in which many of us are called to form the functional dimension of our spiritual life; to gain in ego-strength and in rational-critical ability; to establish a niche in society from which we can serve humanity. It is a time of commitment; a time also of functional asceticism, of detachment from fantasy and acceptance of divinely ordained reality. It can be a graced, rewarding, stimulating period. The richest development of functional skills may take place in the 30's; these years may be marked also by a concrete realization of earlier ideals and projects.

However, preoccupation with practical thought can lead to neglect of symbolic-poetic thought. Increasing responsibility can take its toll and give rise to negative feelings.

Around the age of 40, many attain their highest acuity and greatest functional output. They feel that they still have at their disposal vital resources of abundant energy and physical well being. This explains the slogan: "Life begins at 40."

As we will see, some time after 40 for certain people the mid-life crisis may announce itself. This crisis is one pronounced instance of the various transcendence crises we are called to in life. It will bring about a turning point that may spell a radical change in the ongoing formation of many people, who have perhaps neglected their spiritual growth in previous phases of development.

Chapter III

TRANSCENDENCE CRISES AND THE MID-LIFE MODEL

Second Phase of the Mid-Years

The second phase of the mid-years may fall approximately between 44 and 55. For a number of people in our culture it is marked by a more pronounced occurrence of the transcendence crises which initiate new forms of spiritual life in the history of our human development. Such a specific transcendence crisis at this time of life is often called the mid-life crisis, in spite of the fact that it happens for some people earlier, in more gradual, less dramatic forms. In many it may take place later in life or not at all. This crisis, if it happens in this period of life, may be initiated by a loss of vitality, diminishment of opportunity and physical changes. At the same time the transcendent dimension of our spiritual life begins to announce itself, especially when we neglected it before. It begins to emerge as an invitation to deeper spiritual formation. This does not mean that the vital and functional dimensions should not continue their role. They surely should but in subordination to the more explicit manifestations of transcendent aspirations. Similarly, the transcendent dimension of the spiritual life should have been active in the period of functional formation. The less this was the case, the more dramatic the role of this specific transcendence crisis in our life may be.

Crisis: Danger and Opportunity

Crisis, from the Greek *krineo,* means literally a parting of the ways. The mid-life crisis — like any transcendence crisis — denotes a parting of life directions. The option lies between a central functional and a central transcendent direction of our spiritual formation. We may have to make up for the many more gradual transcendence crises we have ignored or repressed earlier in life.

Crisis implies also stress and uncertainty. The mid-life crisis may make us tense and anxious: it implies loss of a spiritual life form we felt at home with and the option for one that seems initially alien to us. We are understandably afraid to take this leap into the unknown.

The Chinese have two characters for the word crisis. One character means danger, the other opportunity.

The mid-life transcendence crisis gives rise to many dangers: first, the danger of fixation on the functional level of the spiritual life, or the reverse, the danger of overreaction against the former period, leading to a foolish rejection of functional spirituality and ego-resiliency; second, the danger of opting for a floating quasi-spirituality; third, the danger of past unsolved problems and neuroses that tend to reappear in full strength during a transcendence crisis; fourth, the danger of overactivity, of frantic busy-ness to cover up the greater need for rest and recollection.

Yet any transcendence crisis means also opportunity: the opportunity to become truly human, to discover our unique self as called forth by the Transcendent, to harmonize all dimensions of our life. The opportunities of the transcendence crisis allow for growth in wisdom and inwardness, for coming in touch with our deepest self. The turning point of our life encourages us to take stock of what has been, to ready ourselves for the twilight of advanced age, for death and dying.

A new transcendent look at our past creates room for reconciliation between what we had hoped for or ought to have done and what we did not do; it allows also for reconciliation with people, events and things that marred our healthy self-formation and, therefore, hurt our chances in life.

This crisis helps us to find out how we can meaningfully fill the time left to us before our transition to eternal life, how to age graciously. It also enables us to give more selfless and inspired care to others, even when monetary or professional rewards for such concerns may be less forthcoming than in the past.

Prelude to the Mid-Life Crisis of Transcendence

The crisis can be triggered off in some by a

shocking event: a stroke, a heart attack, an accident, a death in the family, a missed promotion, a marital discord, a run-in with the children. In others the crisis begins slowly, marked by a feeling of waning vitality, of fatigue. For example, a surgeon, who used to be able to stand at the operation table all day without exhaustion, still performs with the same acuity but tires sooner. A tennis player can still deliver three hard sets of singles but is more worn out.

Concern rises to the degree that opportunities for success narrow. The man in the bank realizes in his late 30's or early 40's that he probably will not become the head of his department, certainly not the president. The somewhat grandiose visions of earlier years begin to fade.

A woman discovers gray hair, wrinkles and often loses her youthful appearance. The prettier she is the more painful is the diminishment of attention. Losing her looks can be as distressing for a woman as lost economic opportunities are for a man.

The crisis deepens. Boredom sets in. It is as if nothing exciting ever happens any more; it feels like I'm dying on the vine. Should I do something else? Should I do things differently? Am I trapped in my marriage, my profession? Why stay with it? An affair, another marriage may open new avenues. We question our roles and commitments, our religious affiliations. Perhaps we felt fine as punctual Christians, well informed about our faith, observant of its rites and regulations. Now our conviction seems to evaporate. Religion does not attract us as before. If rites and rules are all religion has to offer, why go on with it? Disenchantment may grow to a crisis of faith, a questioning of beliefs.

A crisis in our life of intimacy may follow. Some fall in love for the first time. Others experience a crush on another man or woman. They try to regain the vital power they feel slipping away, to recoup passion before it is gone forever. Our new love seems to harbor the secret of vitality. We yearn to prove to ourselves and others that we are still potent and attractive.

The decline of ambitions opens a door to other longings. Forgotten needs come tumbling out, together with a reawakening of sensitivity, fantasy and playfulness; it all may end in an explosion of desire. The result: a heightened vulnerability for new opportunities of intimacy.

Paradoxically, falling in love may be fuelled also by the first glimmers of transcendent life. Vague longings for serenity, for goodness, truth and beauty, for union, may rise up in consciousness. These longings express a hidden search for the mystery of the Transcendent. Unfortunately, at the beginning of this crisis the person is usually not ready for the experience of this mystery. What does one do with such yearnings? Before we realize what is happening, they become focused on someone who appears as a symbol of all that is good, true, and beautiful. Unrecognized aspirations can nourish a sudden love for an attractive human being.

Crisis may arise not only in our marriage, faith and

commitments but also in our professional life. Is our work really that valuable? Are there any opportunities left to make our mark? We have grown accustomed to the position we reached; it no longer seems that fulfilling.

Often the crisis of illness strikes us at this time. High blood pressure, arthritis, blood vessel disease, ulcers or heart attack confront us with our vulnerability.

In the midst of all this, we face a crisis of detachment. Grandparents, parents, friends or colleagues die. The nearer they were to us, the more we experience their death as a loss of part of ourselves. They are a reminder that we shall die too. We feel unsettled at the thought of how finite our life really is.

Crisis of Confinement

All of these experiences precipitate the crisis of confinement. The English word *confinement* comes from the Latin *confinis* that means bordering. *Finis* in *confinis* refers to border, frontier, limit. Hence our word confinement means an experience of confining or being confined; restrained within doors, for example, by illness.

In our mid-life transcendence crisis we begin to feel how confined we are within the limits of shrinking opportunities — of our life span, our vital and functional capacities, our intimate relationships with others. The experience of confinement makes us aware of our finiteness. We have read about human finitude in books, articles, catechisms. We heard about it in sermons. In retreats we were reminded of the fleetingness of life. We understood this fact intellectually; we believed it, but it did not touch us; we knew it but we did not feel it. The finitude of our life becomes an *experiential* awareness in the mid-life crisis. We become aware of it in our experience of confinement.

The mid-life crisis of transcendence is thus negatively: the disclosure of our finiteness in the very experience of our confinement manifested to us by a loss of opportunities, relationships, vital and functional strength and endurance.

A hormonal imbalance in our body chemistry confines control of the vital life. A woman goes through menopause; a man suffers a less drastic change in a previously stable internal organization. A decline in energy and physical power results. Some suffer headaches, vertigo, fatigue, restlessness, insomnia, backaches, ulcers, skin rashes, hot flashes. While many symptoms may be related to the psychological problems of this period, they demonstrate in unmistakable body language how confined we are by our aging organism.

Psychological symptoms of the mid-life crisis make us aware how our power of self-control is confined by feelings we cannot immediately rise above. At times we feel depressed. We realize some causes of our depression like the diminishment of opportunity, the dissolution of dreams and ideals. There is something more, something intangible, we cannot put our finger on. The deeper awareness of our finitude is in the background of our depression. But it is difficult to pinpoint finitude. The same for vague anxiety. Concretely we fear we may never reach the ideals, directives and projects we set up for ourselves. We are afraid that life may end up less significant than we dreamt it to be. A free floating uneasiness pervades our consciousness. A dim awareness of being enclosed in our contingency is the deepest source of this anxiety.

We grieve about the confines of youthful vigor. We mourn the passing of young adulthood. It pains us that at 40 more than half of life seems to be over.

To see ourselves crumbling before our eyes leads to self doubt. Repeatedly we ask: Am I good at my work? Can I still create, produce? Can I compete with younger employees? Am I able to hold the attention of my husband or wife? Do I still look worthwhile or attractive to my children and friends? We feel the limits of our capacity to impress others.

Frustration results. We become irritable. Angry tempers flare up. Some withdraw in a shell; others try to escape in frantic busy-ness. Housewives clean their homes too much and too eagerly. It is easier to busy oneself than to face contingency and confinement. This situation is vividly described in the following excerpt from *A Confession and What I Believe* by Leo Tolstoy:

> So I lived; but five years ago something very strange began to happen to me. At first I experienced

moments of perplexity and arrest of life, as though I did not know how to live or what to do; and I felt lost and became dejected. But this passed, and I went on living as before. Then these moments of perplexity began to recur oftener and oftener, and always in the same form. They were always expressed by the questions: What's it for? What does it lead to?

At first it seemed to me that these were aimless and irrelevant questions. I thought that it was all well known, and that if I should ever wish to deal with the solution, it would not cost me much effort; just at present I had no time for it, but when I wanted to I should be able to find the answer. The questions, however, began to repeat themselves frequently, and more and more insistently to demand replies; and like drops of ink always falling on one place, they ran together into one black blot.

That occurred which happens to every one sickening with a mortal internal disease. At first trivial signs of indisposition appear, to which the sick man pays no attention; then these signs reappear more and more often and merge into one uninterrupted period of suffering. The suffering increases, and before the sick man can look around, what he took for a mere indisposition has already become more important to him than anything else in the world — it is death!

That was what happened to me. I understood that it was no casual indisposition, but something very important, and that if these questions constantly repeated themselves, they would have to be answered. And I tried to answer them. The questions seemed such stupid, simple, childish questions; but as soon as I touched them and tried to solve them, I at once became convinced (1) that they are not childish and stupid, but the most important and profound of life's questions; and (2) that, try as I would, I could not solve them. Before occupying myself with my Samara estate, the education of my son, or the writing of a book, I had to know *why* I was doing it. As long as I did not know why, I could do nothing, and could not live. Amid the thoughts of estate management which greatly occupied me at that time, the question would suddenly occur to me: "Well, you will have 6,000 desyatinas of land in Samara Government and 300 horses, and what next?" . . . And I was quite disconcerted, and did not know what to think. Or, when considering my plans for the education of my children, I would say to myself: "What for?" Or when considering how the peasants might become prosperous, I suddenly said to myself: "But what does it matter to me?" Or when thinking of the fame my works would bring me, I said to myself: "Very well; you will be more famous than Gogol or Pushkin or Shakespeare or Moliere, or than all the writers in the world — and what of it?" And I could find no reply at all. The questions would not wait, they had to be answered at once, and if I did not answer them, it was impossible to live. But there was no answer.

I felt that what I had been standing on had collapsed, and that I had nothing left under my feet. What I had lived on no longer existed; and I had nothing left to live on.

My life came to a standstill. I could breathe, eat, drink, and sleep, and I could not help doing these things; but there was no life, for there were no wishes the fulfilment of which I could consider reasonable. If I desired anything, I knew in advance that whether I satisfied my desire or not, nothing would come of it. Had a fairy come and offered to fulfil my desires I should not have known what to ask. If in moments of intoxication I felt something which, though not a wish, was a habit left by former wishes, in sober moments I knew this to be a delusion, and that there was really nothing to wish for. I could not even wish to know the truth, for I guessed of what it consisted. The truth was that life is meaningless. I had, as it were, lived, lived and walked, walked, till I had come to a precipice and saw clearly that there was nothing ahead of me but destruction. It was impossible to stop, impossible to go back, and impossible to close my eyes or avoid seeing that there was nothing ahead but suffering and real death — complete annihilation.

It had come to this, that I, a healthy, fortunate man, felt I could no longer live: some irresistible power impelled me to rid myself one way or other of life. I cannot say I wished to kill myself. The power which drew me away from life was stronger, fuller, and more widespread than any mere wish. It was a force similar to the former striving to live, only in a contrary direction. All my strength drew me away from life. The thought of self-destruction now came to me as naturally as thoughts of how to improve my life had come formerly. And it was so seductive that I had to be wily with myself lest I should carry it out too hastily. I did not wish to hurry, only because I wanted to use all efforts to disentangle the matter. "If I cannot unravel matters, there will always be time." And it was then that I, a man favoured by fortune, hid a cord from myself, lest I should hang myself from the crosspiece of the partition in my room, where I undressed alone every evening; and I ceased to go out shooting with a gun, lest I should be tempted by so easy a way of ending my life. I did not myself know what I wanted: I feared life, desired to escape from it; yet still hoped something of it.

And all this befell me at a time when all around me

I had what is considered complete good fortune. I was not yet fifty; I had a good wife who loved me and whom I loved, good children, and a large estate which without much effort on my part improved and increased. I was respected by my relations and acquaintances and more than at any previous time. I was praised by others, and without much self-deception could consider that my name was famous. And far from being insane or mentally diseased, I enjoyed on the contrary a strength of mind and body such as I have seldom met with among men of my kind; physically, I could keep up with the peasants at mowing, and mentally I could work for eight and ten hours at a stretch without experiencing any ill results from such exertion. And in this situation I came to this — that I could not live, and, fearing death, had to employ cunning with myself to avoid taking my own life.

My mental condition presented itself to me in this way: my life is a stupid and spiteful joke some one has played on me. Though I did not acknowledge a "some one" who created me, yet such a presentation — that some one had played an evil and stupid joke on me by placing me in the world — was the form of expression that suggested itself most naturally to me.

Involuntarily it appeared to me that there, somewhere, was some one who amused himself by watching how I lived for thirty or forty years; learning, developing, maturing in body and mind, and how — having with matured mental powers reached the summit of life from which it all lay before me, I stood on that summit — like an arch-fool — seeing clearly that there is nothing in life, and that there has been and will be nothing. And he was amused . . .

But whether that "some one" laughing at me

existed or not, I was none the better off. I could give no reasonable meaning to any single action, or to my whole life. I was only surprised that I could have avoided understanding this from the very beginning — it has been so long known to all. To-day or to-morrow sickness and death will come (they had come already) to those I love or to me; nothing will remain but stench and worms. Sooner or later my affairs, whatever they may be, will be forgotten, and I shall not exist. Then why go on making any effort? . . . How can man fail to see this? And how go on living? That is what is surprising! One can only live while one is intoxicated with life; as soon as one is sober it is impossible not to see that it is all a mere fraud and a stupid fraud! That is precisely what it is: there is nothing either amusing or witty about it: it is simply cruel and stupid.*

Main Questions of the Mid-Life Transcendence Crisis

What does life mean? Where am I going? What form do I give to my life? These questions express human aspirations for meaning, direction, formation. They are basic questions, operative at all age levels, only now we become more aware of them. At this turning point of life we take stock of the past; we look to the future. This brings such basic questions to the surface and forces them to the forefront of our attention.

The questions and their answers are related to one

---

*Trans. Aylmer Maude (London: Oxford University Press, 1921), pp. 18-23.

another. To give form to our life we have to know in what direction we should go. To find that direction we should find out what life is all about, what its meaning is. Logically, therefore, questions concerning the meaning of life should come first; those of direction and formation should follow.

In practice, however, the question of direction arises first in a transcendence crisis. We look into the past. Where did we go? What direction did our life take? Why is this direction disrupted? We look towards the future. How are we to fill the days left to us? We become aware of our own death as an imminent possibility.

Questioning makes us wonder what did we make of our life so far? Did we give it the form we intended to? Have there been problems that made it difficult for our life to take shape? Can we resolve these problems now? Problems arise in relation to contingency and detachment, expectations and ideals, direction and continuity of life, daily activity and appearance. How did ideals, dreams, desires, duties and relationships form or deform us? How do we deal with that as yet unresolved part of life?

The second half of life is given to most of us to solve what can be solved, to make up for delayed formation, and to reconcile ourselves with what cannot be altered.

We hope that the remainder of our life will grant us more wholeness and depth than the past, that it will integrate former developments and prepare us for our final transition.

What gives rise to these basic questions for many who ignored or repressed them earlier in life is the detachment forced upon us during the second half of mid-life. Being detached from many things dear to us, things intertwined with our life and selfhood, may lead to an experience of crisis. This crisis is permeated by basic questions and manifests itself in many ways. Each aspect of the crisis is almost a crisis of its own. In some sense the mid-life crisis of transcendence is not one but many crises, all united by the same basic questions.

Once detachment is forced upon us, many of us may feel compelled to interact with that unexpected reality. Out of this interaction emerge the subcrises of, respectively, contingency, inner detachment, expectation, direction, continuity, idealized life directives, appearances, de-activation, and ultimate meaning.

In the chapters to follow, we shall first consider the experience of forced detachment in the second half of life. Then we shall give separate attention to each of the subsequent crisis aspects, enumerated above.

Chapter IV

DETACHMENT IN THE SECOND HALF OF LIFE

In this period people, things and experiences dear to us become detached from our life. Detachment may be from position and opportunity; from health, skill and energy; from familiar buildings and surroundings; from trusted customs replaced by others in church and society; from parenthood when a child leaves home; from parents, family members, friends and colleagues taken away from us. We lose someone or something that has become part of the fabric of our life during these 40 or so years. The loss is irreplaceable; it cuts deeply and detaches radically. We feel stripped. It takes time to realize that this cutting of ties frees us for inner growth. We gain spiritually by losing humanly. But we grow only when external detachment is accepted inwardly, when it is complemented by inner detachment.

Experiences that meant most to us become tenuous. Weariness takes over; daily duties become oppressive. We do not find as much fun in life. Ambitions collapse. Out of sheer duty we keep doing what we have to do, going where we are supposed to go. We push ourselves through days that seem gray and endless.

Having passed the halfway point of life, we are closer to death than to birth. A sense of life's confinement begins to permeate our days. We feel threatened by inadequacy and failure. Our enthusiasm seems atrophied.

A woman visited me in the throes of the mid-life crisis. She poured out her fear, doubt and frustration. She berated herself for her dark outlook and discouragement not realizing how natural that can be in this stage of transition.

"I don't know what has come over me. I felt everything was going well. I am single, but I enjoyed my job. I cared for my nephews and nieces. I was the aunt they liked most. Now they have grown up. I don't see much of them anymore.

"At the job, younger girls seem better than I with the customers. They look so much more attractive. I can see that the men like them better than me. I'm surely not what I used to be. I feel kind of old and crabby these days.

"I look at these young things and feel like hiding under the counter. What have I done with my life?, I ask myself.

"I've done good things. I've worked hard. I was good to my family, did a lot for my nephews and nieces, contributed to our church but I could have done more. I feel so down at times I could kick myself.

"I know it sounds stupid, but I sometimes get the

feeling my family doesn't really like me in spite of all I've done for them. They tell me they care for me, but do they mean it? Sometimes I feel the need for a good cry. I know I exaggerate; they are not that bad. I suppose they are busy with their own lives.

"Sometimes I think soon I will be retired from the store. Then things will get better. I can do what I like. But I am not so sure. If I feel useless now, what will it be like when I lose my job? The only thing I can wait for is dying. My whole life runs before me like a movie and I say to myself: has that been all? What was the use of it? What does it all mean anyway?"

This woman expresses the despair that can overwhelm us in this crisis. We hide it well. We keep up appearances and maintain a good front: "Everything is just dandy." But we weep inwardly and nobody seems to know or care. One man told me, "I was alone in my office. I did not get the promotion and the raise in salary I had worked so hard for. A younger man was promoted over my head. I had given so much of my time to the job that my wife and kids did not know me any longer. My marriage was a mess. And now this. Had it all been for nothing? Then and there it dawned on me that my time was over. Others were going to advance, but I would rust in my little cubby hole. Nobody would give a damn, least of all my family. I felt so down I was tempted to make an end to it. But that evening there was an office party. I clowned my way through it, showing nothing."

"Showing nothing." In these words we feel the strain of pulling ourselves together, the weight of the masks we carry into mid-life, the strain of our refusal to shed at least some of them, like the pretense that we are much younger and stronger than we really are. We may no longer know what is appearance and what is truly us? In the flurry of finding our life direction when we were younger, we covered up our real self. Now we ask ourselves, bewildered, what is the cover and what is me? The jolt of the crisis makes us realize that we have lost touch with our center, that we are more lived by others than living our own lives. Appearances increasingly fail to evoke the appreciation we want so badly. We have to find in our own deeper self what we detect less and less in the world that surrounds us. Shedding masks, giving up appearances that were precious to us, is part of the asceticism of the middle years. We have to shed the mask of importance, of invulnerability, of omniscience, of pride and one-upmanship. When we cease to compete, we may become our real selves, at least in the second half of life.

Experience of the Death of Others

Around this time of life many of us experience the loss of a friend, colleague, parent, child or other family member. It affects the crisis of detachment and deepens its intensity. The death of a loved one can have a shattering impact on the living. It takes us out of our complacent routine and compels us to look beyond our projects, to ask about life itself. A death in the family cannot be avoided. Our own life and the form it has taken is being questioned.

The departure of a dear one makes a deep incision. The closer the loved one was, the deeper it cuts. The cut may be healed but always it leaves a scar. We feel shaken, cast back upon ourselves, reminded of mortality: life will not go on forever. Other mid-life experiences may confirm this feeling of futility; anxiety rises in us.

The death of a loved one is a dying to something within us. It can bring about an awareness of the deeper core of our being: of what lasts when everything is lost. Within that core a transcendent ground may be disclosed to us.

Mary paces her living room in shock. Her husband had a heart attack. The ambulance came to take him to the hospital but he died on the way. Panic overtakes her as she tries to deny the unbelievable. Anxiety comes tumbling in. Her mind is overcome with questions. How did it happen? Why him? What will become of her? What to do now? Slowly it dawns upon her that John is no more. Tomorrow is bleak and unreal.

The first weeks she pines away in loneliness, lingering on the verge of despair. Empty days and nights leave her numb and yearning. Through a wilderness of feelings the questions keep racing back. Can things ever be the same? How can she go on without him? Who will support her, love her, encourage her? Is life worth living?

After years of togetherness the void is dreadful. With the passing of time, Mary begins to delve more deeply into the emptiness that fences her in. Is there some meaning to John's leaving? Life without him is elusive yet it has to be lived. But why and how? Is sorrow useless? What form can she give to the remaining years?

In the long, lonely evenings Mary begins to face the mystery of death. It is strangely interwoven with life. She realizes as never before: all have to die; everything and every person is finite. You are sure of nothing. Loss is always around the corner. Life's journey is a bit by bit dying to what is dear to us. She senses she has to work the separation through on a deeper level. She must accept her grief, allow herself to really feel it. The task of inner detachment is necessary. Gradually the mist begins to clear; there are moments of resignation that fade away again. But the moments stay longer and longer. Mary vacillates between her grief and a revival of interest in people around her. One day she wants to be all by herself; the next she feels like finding her way back to work, friends and social commitments.

These ups and downs allow her to assimilate slowly the truth that mid-life teaches: life is contingent, unpredictable and finite for all of us. It has to be accepted and lived in its contingency, with zest and detachment. We can be sure of nothing and yet love everything. The only thing we are sure of is our own inmost self rooted in the mystery of divine compassion. That mystery sustains us, yet does not take away the beauty and the curse of freedom. We are responsible for our life and feelings. Neither does this mysterious presence remove the detachments contingency and mortality impose on us.

Mary's formation crisis is centered in the great separation imposed on her. Other detachments deepen its impact. She matures in sorrow. The stark truth of life begins to seep through. No longer does she hide from life's reality. Neither does she try to control it like she did in her late 30's. The threat of separation is tamed while becoming a real part of her being; it is something to live with while making the best of it. She begins to see this threat in the light of faith. Her faith becomes more alive and meaningful; it speaks about ultimate realities. Mary is surprised by the dawn of a security she did not know before. She does not have to deny life as it is. The flight in distraction is no longer necessary. She can live with contingency, expect detachment and accept it quietly. She knows how to give meaning to loss from the center of her being. She has come of age. Before that crisis much of her life had been a flight from the harshness of reality into frantic functioning. Mary realizes that mid-age maturity means a turning from flight to the facing of reality.

Chapter V

CRISES OF CONTINGENCY, DETACHMENT, EXPECTATION AND DIRECTION

Contingency Crisis

Mary went through a "contingency experience." Such experiences are crucial. The way we respond to them affects the outcome of the mid-life transcendence crisis.

According to Webster, contingency means the fact of existing as an individual human being in time; dependent on others for existence; menaced by death; dependent on oneself for the course and quality of existence.

Our life is contingent. We are never sure that things will go right for us; that we will survive another day in good health; that family and friends will remain faithful in their affection or stay well themselves; that status, power, possession will last; that our life will not be affected by war, depression, illness or confusion. The list is endless. To function well we try not to think about such calamities. We fear that negative thoughts may interfere with our effective performance. Accordingly in the functional phase of life, for many of us in the 30's and early 40's, the awareness of our contingency may reach an all time low. At the end of this period, however, the mid-life transcendence crisis may be initiated by contingency experiences we can no longer deny. The functionality of the former period acted as a defense against these experiences. The lessening of functioning, the diminishment of achievement opportunities, leaves, as it were, cracks in this armor.

Each phase of spiritual formation has its own specific formative assignment. In mid-life the task for many of us is to transform the negative impact of the contingency experience into a positive one.

Not every contingency experience is critical enough to compel awareness of the precariousness of life and performance. Losing some money, failing an exam, suffering a headache may not trigger off a transcendence crisis. Other experiences, such as the sudden death of Mary's husband, children leaving home, a stroke, render us startlingly aware of the vulnerability of our human position. They are breakthrough experiences. Their shattering force pierces the armor of functionality. We call them *foundational* contingency experiences. They belong to the fundamental conditions for any breakthrough to a deeper form of life. They make us free for a transcendent outlook on life and world. Contingency experiences challenge us to look beyond the "cozy cubby holes" we have dug for ourselves in society. They teach us that success is pervaded with failure, perfection with imperfection, skill with deficiency, life with death, joy with sadness, pleasure with pain, affection with indifference, love with hate, possession with loss, initiative with risk, health with illness.

When the contingency experience strikes, we feel shaken, cast back upon ourselves. We try to deny the experience, to carry on as if nothing has happened. To succeed is really to lose out on the opportunities for rebirth a transcendence crisis offers. The more shattering our experience the greater the opportunity. For resurrection to happen we must acknowledge the finitude this experience points to. This is a first aspect of the mid-life formation task. The second aspect is to grow to reconciliation with the contingency of life. Such reconciliation makes us realistic, resolute and decisive.

The direction of the remainder of our life is influenced by our acceptance of contingency. Contingency makes us aware of what we may still attain. We do not raise our expectations too high. We accept our limits and those of our life situation; we do not try to outdo ourselves. The exaltation of youth is replaced by the sobriety of age. Neither do we give in to defeatism when our more sober projects are thwarted by opposition, disappointment, unforeseeable loss of health, skill or opportunity. We feel at home with failure and vulnerability. We adapt our projects quietly and go on from there.

This endurance of contingency, this perseverance in service of humanity, points to a deeper motivation. Before this time our motivation may have drawn mainly on vital drives and functional ambitions; now its main source is transcendent aspirations and inspirations. We face here a third aspect of the mid-life formation task: the transformation of our motivational life. Such transformation is possible only via an opening up to the Transcendent in faith, hope, and love. We relocate our certitude in the Transcendent, in the divine image within. He becomes our aspiration and inspiration. Our care for others becomes an act of love for the unique image of the Transcendent each of them is called to become. He becomes our reward and our forgiveness.

Contingency experiences happened to us also before the mid-life crisis. Our right response to them helped us gain in transcendence, resoluteness and realism. But these periodic conversions to transcendence were in many lives not so radical as the conversion in mid-life may be. For a number of us they were perhaps no more than preparatory exercises for the transformation of the mid-life crisis. Their absence would make it difficult to cope with the shattering experiences mid-life may bring us. We would have no experiences to fall back upon; no strategies of transformation that helped us overcome the minor crises we faced before. The prognosis is poor for those who did not have any of these minor transcendence crises or who did not work them through creatively. They may need spiritual direction, counseling or psychotherapy.

We are inclined to evade the contingency experience because it brings dread to the surface. Initially it causes disharmony and uneasiness. A secret anxiety to die may rise in some of us. Our self-consistency is broken up. We experience powerlessness, a temporary loss of balance. Naturally we try to rid ourselves of such painful feelings, to regain a comfortable and manageable functionality. This control grants us a make-believe feeling of security. We cope with the experience and apparently solve its threat, but it may return in other forms, haunting us to the end of our days.

The repression of the contingency experience leaves us more vulnerable than before. We have to spend added energy to keep it underground. This means that every new contingency experience will give rise to more anxiety and pressure. There will be no liberation until we decide to take the risk, to face our contingency. We may take the leap to a more transcendent life only when we see not merely its danger but also its possible gain.

Detachment Crisis

Detachment is indispensable in self-formation. It happens to us from birth to death. Detachment can be passive and external or active and internal. Passive detachment involves the deprivation of something dear to us. It happens whether we like it or not, whether we accept or refuse it. The consequences can be formative or deformative. It depends on how we respond to our deprivation. Here active detachment comes in. Active detachment implies giving up inwardly our attachment to what has been taken away from us or to what we relinquished freely. Active detachment implies a working through of our feelings about deprivation. This working through consists of a phase of mourning, a phase of redirection of our feelings, and a final phase of reintegration of our life.

What detachment is for one person may involve no detachment for another. It depends on what personal meaning deprivation has for us. People in some Asiatic cultures, for example, are concerned mostly about loss of honor or "loss of face." Even accidental failures in administrative matters, that one is not guilty of, are experienced as a loss of face. The victims may resign their job in shame. Americans would see such an event as one of those failings we all have to live with.

Detachment always plays a role in the spiritual formation of the person. Some periods of life, however, are marked by detachment more than others. Any transcendence crisis is such a period. In fact it could be called a crisis of detachment.

Detachment in mid-life often implies other detachments. For example, children detach their lives from that of their parents when they leave home to start their own families. Their leaving leads to a loss of liveliness, a diminishment of companionship in the home, a lessening of the parents' role as home makers and providers. The parental "need to be needed" has to find other outlets. Their "current form of life" has to change.

The core form of our personality is more or less lasting. Around that core we form a "current form of life." This current self consists of attitudes, social roles, self-images, skills, sensitivities, and projects. They are in tune with our present capacities; they also respond to the actual tasks and situations the Lord allows us to be challenged by. Both our capacities and our life situations are in a process of change in the mid-life crisis. As a result many aspects of our current life form are in jeopardy. We are invited to detach ourselves from the charm, strength, dignity, and independence that may mark our current self image. We have to find these qualities back on a deeper level of selfhood. They must now become rooted in the transcendent value of our core self. This core is more lasting; it is less dependent on our vital-functional strength, less touched by the approval or disapproval of our environment.

Because our situation changes in the second half of mid-life, our current self has to change too. We must develop a new current life form more in tune with our core form and yet responding to the demands of the new situations we have to face.

The asceticism of mid-life thus implies inner detachment. The older we are the more detachment may cost us. We invested many years of discipline, adaptation and hard work in the formation of our current life form. An example of this would be job performance. Say I have become an excellent salesman. It took years of struggle to develop self-assurance, flexible adaptation to customers, a charming approach, a clever sales pitch, and the ability to endure complaints and demands. All these qualities have become a part of my current form of life. Now I am slipping. They give me an office job or suggest early retirement. Some of the traits that made up my current self as salesman are no longer useful in my new position. People find them phony. After all I don't have to sell them anything. Thinking about it, I may say to myself: "Maybe my way was phony. Perhaps my charm did not come from the heart; it was possibly more a trick than a virtue. Yet I invested so much energy, pride and perseverance in the acquisition of this charm that I don't like to give it up." I hate to see that part of me fading away. To give it up is like dying a little. I cannot yet see that my surface charm needs to be replaced by a deeper kind of charm, rooted in love of God and others.

Another example could be found in the mother of many children who is left alone when all of them have gone their way. She has developed attitudes of care, skills of cleaning and cooking; she is good at counseling, entertaining, creating a homey atmosphere. These performances and attitudes made up her current life form as a caring mother and effective housekeeper. Now all seems changed. She must transform her current self into one that is less busy around the home, more geared to the care of an aging husband; their shared life is more solitary than in the days when friends of the children dropped in, challenging her capacity to dream up a fast meal for more people than expected. But it took her so much time to become an effective mother that detachment from these endeavors is hard to take. Frustration is unavoidable.

Inner detachment implies also detachment from emotional investments. It involves a divesting that makes us free for a deeper investment in transcendent values.

Expectation Crisis

The mid-life transcendence crisis is not only one of actual but of expected detachments. Seeing what happens to aging family members, neighbors, friends, and colleagues, we begin to expect that the same will happen to us. Part of human living is what we could call a life of expectation. During the functional development of our spiritual life, we lived in the expectation of ongoing promotion, a steady increase in skill, success and social significance. The mid-life transcendence crisis threatens this life of expectation. We expect instead the detachments that begin to manifest themselves in the lives of many around us. These threats may add up in our mind to a basic threat to survival. Indeed the survival of our current life form is at stake. We do not as yet realize that our current self is not our whole self. The death of the present self makes the disclosure of the deeper self possible. This disclosure influences the formation of richer current selves in the last half of life.

One of the first aspects of our selfhood to be touched by the mid-life crisis is thus our life of expectations. We begin to sense how attached we are to many things we have taken for granted. We do not want to part with them. We grieve over what we may lose in the future. The deeper our investment in those threatened aspects of our current form of life, the more intense our fear.

Detachment is in some way interwoven with self-emergence. Our deepest self can only come to the fore when we die to attachments that obscure the transcendent values waiting to reveal themselves.

Mid-Life Detachment and Asceticism

The rhythm of attachment and detachment has marked all of our life. From infancy on we had to give up things we had an emotional investment in. Some were taken away from us; others we gave up freely. A relaxed asceticism may have taught us to "offer things up" in service of higher values. These exercises in detachment were called mortifications; we "died a little" to rise to a stronger, deeper life. If we were fortunate, the meaning of detachment in our life might have been illumined by the symbolism of the great religions.

In Christianity, for instance, detachment is linked with our dying and rising in Christ, celebrated daily in the Eucharist and highlighted in the liturgy of Lent and Easter. The mid-life transcendence crisis is, as it were, the Easter mystery at the heart of our life cycle. It is the "lent of life." The threat of multiple detachments from what is dear to us overwhelms us as Jesus was overwhelmed by the threat of suffering and death in the Garden of Gethsemane. For Jesus the threat itself was agony; it made him cry out: Father, let this chalice pass by, if it is your will.

The detachment crisis of mid-life is not like the

small detachments we went through in other stages of self-emergence. Still, a recall of how we gave meaning to smaller deprivations can help us rekindle the significance that sustained us in the past. We have to deepen this meaning now that we face more decisive detachments. If we were not blessed with ascetical training in childhood and youth, the later transcendence crises will be more difficult to cope with. Yet we should not despair. Available to all of us is the symbolism of the great religions of humanity that sustained the mid-life journey of countless generations.

The Christian believes that the symbols of his faith point not only to the reality they signify but convey it graciously. Christ's agony does not remain outside us. The mystery of His passion permeates our mid-life journey and the agonies it may entail for some of us. The grace of this presence enables us to transcend detachments. The mid-life transcendence crisis is a kind of dark night of the soul we may have to go through. At the end of the tunnel, the light of resurrection dawns. The second half of life is meant to be celebration of our newly emerging self in the Risen Lord.

Detachment abounds in everyday life. Due to distractions, it often goes unnoticed. Detachment, however, can no longer be taken for granted in a transcendence crisis. It breaks in upon us with violence. This break-in is meant to become a breakthrough. It is first of all an opening up to a new life direction. To understand this aspect of any transcendence crisis, we must examine what spiritual direction means in our life. Only then can we appreciate what a disruption of direction implies and how a transcendence crisis ensues from it.

Direction Crisis

We all feel naturally inclined to give some form to our lives and our surroundings. The direction of this formation is partly chosen by us, partly imposed on us. We find our life form by interacting with our culture. But we cannot modify our culture at will. There are certain things we cannot change. Many directives for our life are already present in the culture into which we are born. They limit our possibilities of self-formation. Our own capacities are limited too. They pose another restriction on our power of formation. The divine direction of our life is thus for a great part conveyed to us in the limits put upon our capacities and our surroundings. Initially we are not even aware that our life has a direction. Direction is given to our life implicitly while we interact daily with people, events and things that co-constitute our life situation.

We spoke earlier of our life of expectation. Expectation is an essential part of direction. While interacting with our surroundings, we look towards the future. Doing so we develop certain expectations; they too give direction to our lives. For example, the man who starts a candy shop has to involve himself in daily sales and promotion schemes. Yet at the same time he cannot stop thinking about what the future may bring. Should he buy more or better candies? At what prices? How can he attract steady customers? Can he expand his business? Or should he perhaps be satisfied with what he has and use his remaining time and energy for other hobbies or for family life? He knows he cannot control the future, but he is spontaneously aware that planning and action might modify the direction of his life.

This everyday life direction is taken for granted by the average person. He does not question the process of direction; he simply lives it. As long as right directives flow spontaneously over into daily living, things are unproblematic. Deeper reflection on where we are going seems unnecessary, rather a hindrance than a help. Still our familiar flow of life is pervaded by uncertainty. It is always open to question.

How does our life find its direction? This direction ensues from the daily directives that emerge out of our interaction with our environment. Another source is the directives communicated to us by parents, teachers, preachers, friends, colleagues, neighbors and the media. These represent a fund of sedimented cultural directives. Because of both, we have, as it were, a stock of life directives at hand. Out of this stock we fashion spontaneously our daily life direction. Each time we have to meet a challenge in life, we fall back on this stock of directives to find which ones can best help us. Our life direction develops in experimentation with the directives available to us out of this stock. Every time a directive meets the situation we are in, it is confirmed as an effective part of our life direction.

Sooner or later, however, we will meet problems we cannot solve with the life directives familiar to us. The taken-for-granted effectiveness of our life direction is interrupted; the unproblematic becomes problematic, the unquestioned is questioned. Shocked by the insufficiency of our guidelines, we turn to others for help.

In response to this need all great spiritualities developed modes of "spiritual direction" to be practiced by well prepared directors either in "direction-in-common" or in "private direction."* The word *spiritual* direction highlights the fact that the problem of a halted life direction can be solved only by taking a transcendent stand outside the actual situation and the familiar stock of directives already available. Our human ability to take that distance resides in our unique capacity to transcend immediate data and experiences.

For many of us it takes a transcendence crisis to become aware of the insufficiency of our familiar life directives. They no longer enable us to cope with new complexities. We encounter threats of detachment we never faced in the past nor reflected upon. When we were younger we observed sickness, death, loss of employment, and aging in others. We did not really

---

*See Adrian van Kaam, *Dynamics of Spiritual Self Direction* (Denville, N.J.: Dimension Books, Inc., 1976).

share these events; we were like spectators looking at them but not personally involved in them.

The experiences of a transcendence crisis are thus for the most part unfamiliar. We cannot resolve them with the routine responses we used in the past. They can be disruptive and a threat to our stability. Our embeddedness in the everyday functional world is questioned. We experience dread in losing the security of the present. We cannot yet understand that we are invited to discover values that transcend those that prevailed in the past. Our life direction itself needs to be deepened.

A transcendence crisis marks a turning point in our spiritual life. It can halt the unfolding of our spirituality or foster its finest development. Spiritual growth is the harmonious unfolding of our life as a whole; it affects all dimensions of this life. This explains why our psychic resiliency lessens in quality if a crisis of transcendence remains unsolved.

The mid-life transcendence crisis is a point of no return. We cannot return to a spirituality that is prevalently functional and be at peace. We will never again feel wholly at ease with that prevalence. The crisis has released aspirations that will keep disturbing us preconsciously if they are not fulfilled. A mainly functional life, even when backed by a spiritual intention, does not satisfy us after we have experienced its precariousness. The deepest reason is that God calls us to develop our spirituality by phases over a life time. Each phase is meant to foster one specific dimension without excluding the others. The second half of life is marked by the call to let the transcendent dimension prevail while integrating in it the dimensions and articulations of spiritual life we developed earlier. It is the harvest time of life, the time of wholeness and reconciliation, of growing to the fullness of our unique image in Christ.

We should distinguish between the "raw material" out of which the transcendence crisis is made and the "spiritual objective" of this crisis. The various detachments and stresses we have been describing comprise the "raw material." The turning to a prevalence of transcendent values is the spiritual objective of this crisis. It can thus never be solved satisfactorily by solutions to each distinct stress that accompanies each deprivation. We would in that case apply band-aides where surgery is needed; be dealing with symptoms instead of with the crisis itself.

Let us again look at the symptoms. A middle-aged man drives home from work and realizes that he no longer has the vitality of the past. An elderly woman finds herself alone in her home; her children far away, she sighs in boredom. Another, who grew old caring for a sickly father she dearly loved, is devastated by his death, and by the emptiness yawning before her. They all experience unsteadiness; the sense of sureness in life is lost. Their functional roles are changing. Suppose they were wholesome people with a healthy spiritual life. Their functioning was filled with spiritual meaning. Their spirituality found its expression in their functionality. Now they must relinquish in some measure the dominance of this functional expression of their spirituality; they must partly complement it, partly replace it, with a deeper presence. This challenge is an invitation of the Holy Spirit to inner transformation.

The symptoms described above could be lessened by seeking distraction, entertainment, new company and hobbies, physical exercise, tranquillizers. Such symptom-removal is not necessarily bad. It can produce quieting conditions. Such conditions may facilitate the finding of a deeper spiritual direction which is necessary to solve the crisis itself. But if we restrict ourselves to the removal of psychological and physical symptoms, we may basically hold on to what was and deny ourselves the opportunity for spiritual deepening. Only in accepting the task of integration will we be able to age graciously. The promise of greater maturity, awareness and freedom in our spiritual life is well worth the temporary upheaval caused by middle-age deprivations.

Such opportunities for detachment-emergence are woven into the aging process. We tend to see only the pain, not the gain. The pain is there, a manifold detachment and redirection of our life, but so is the gain in wisdom and wholeness.

Chapter VI
CRISES OF CONTINUITY AND OF IDEALIZED LIFE DIRECTIVES

Continuity Crisis

The changes seem so drastic for some of us that we may ask ourselves if we will still be the same after this turning point. What will be left of me? Is there any continuity to my life? Indeed the mid-life crisis can be experienced by many as a crisis of continuity. Crisis refers to a parting of directions. On the crossroads of life we have to make a decision about a parting of the ways of being ourselves. We need to marshal our resources of courage, hope, and adventure. The reorganization does not mean that our previous life direction will be totally eradicated. Our core remains intact. To explain what we mean, we must point out a distinction between our lasting "core self" and our "periodic selves."

A full spiritual life is a well integrated structure of various aspects or dimensions of this life. We call them the historical-cultural, vital, functional, transcendent and pneumatic dimensions. These structural dimensions do not develop all at once. Each unfolds at a different period of our life. We call these periods of development the "temporal dimensions" of our spiritual life to distinguish them from the structural ones. The Holy Spirit uses each of these periods to foster especially the unfolding of one or the other structural dimension of our spirituality without neglecting totally the others. During such a period, one structural aspect — for example, the functional dimension in the first mid-life period — is in the foreground of our attention and self-formation.

Each period of spiritual development gives rise to the formation of a periodic life form which is a specific temporal articulation of our current form of life. The periodic life form is that aspect of our selfhood that develops in response to demands made by a specific period of our life. This periodic form fosters a deeper spiritual growth in one or the other structural dimension of our spirituality.

In the mid-life crisis the dominance of past periodic forms of life is more radically questioned in many people than ever before. As a result, our periodic selfhood may be so much transformed that we do not recognize it any longer. Yet our core self stays relatively the same. What may happen is that we come to a deeper awareness than we had previously of our core self. Many masks are dropped in mid-life; some of them obscured our true life direction, even from our own eyes. As we abdicate these old worlds of meaning, new ones are disclosed to us. The collapse of a periodic life forms leads to a temporary loss of balance. Hesitantly, in the midst of trial and error, a new periodic self begins to emerge. The self is differentiated; then a process of integration sets in. Wholeness is slowly restored. Our new periodic life form — more transcendent in nature — is gradually integrated with the sediments of our former periodic forms of life. These sediments enriched our continuous core self, provided they were compatible with our unique divine life direction. In the course of this process of reconciliation, we became more at home with that deeper core.

True aspects of spirituality gained in former periods of growth are thus not abandoned; they receded temporarily in the background. When the new dimension of spirituality has been sufficiently formed in us, the sediments of the former dimensions emerge again to be reintegrated into the new deeper dimension. For example, the functional dimension of our spirituality, which unfolded in the first phase of mid-life, will return after the mid-life crisis. But it will now be subordinated more explicitly to the transcendent dimension of the spiritual life.

Our core form contains the divine direction the Holy Spirit gives to our life as a whole; it is the mystery of the unique image of God in which we are created. Our heart knows a direction our intelligence cannot fathom by itself alone. The mid-life crisis is an invitation to listen more to our heart. Listening quietly enables us to see that some former ways of presence are no longer compatible with the divine direction our heart reveals to us.

This deepening awareness of our true self-direction

gives rise to a fresh project of self-formation. We become ready to form a new periodic self. This creation will be more in tune with the unique divine image or form at the core of our being. Mid-life transformation implies a giving up of former modes of presence to people, events and things, as expressed in our current periodic self. Something dies in us and so we must go through a period of mourning. The work of mourning calls for a letting go of what we once cherished as most important. It must give way to values now prevailing in our spiritual life that will result in a new current periodic form of life, dominated by the transcendent and pneumatic self-dimensions.

The task of transition in spirituality thus implies a relativizing of former periods in our spiritual life. We must accept the detachments such relativizing entails; review and evaluate our current life direction; decide which aspects of that direction to deepen and which to abandon; and consider our formative task in the future. Much now present in the current direction of life may have to be abandoned. Still there is much that can be retained as a basis for the formation of a new periodic life form. Each new self-formation should be more in tune with the mystery of divine direction the Holy Spirit gradually reveals in our heart. To be sure much of this process evolves spontaneously and preconsciously without logical deliberation, illumined mostly by the implicit intuitive wisdom of the Spirit. We call this power of the Spirit the pneumatic dimension of our spiritual life.

All detachments bring a sense of loss, a grief for what needs to die in us, an awareness that our final periods of life will not provide fulfillments equal to those of youth and early adulthood. Yet the Spirit grants us also moments of hope, an anticipation of transcendent deepening.

During the mid-life crisis, our former periodic self still has a hold on us. It generates tension and conflict. We experience a yearning for the new while being pulled back into the old. At moments it may seem to some of us that we can move neither forward nor backward, that we are on the verge of drowning. Some may experience a "dark night of the soul" — the threat of chaos and dissolution; the loss of a meaningful life; the powerlessness of former modes of faith. We may feel like repeating with the Lord: My God, my God why have you forsaken me? Toward the end of the crisis we may be drawn to solitude, to a more sober style of faith and prayer. We begin to sense that we are not wholly in line with God's image for our life — that He is calling us to a deeper response.

Gradually it becomes clear that all of our life is a turning to the mystery of our divine life direction. We have to let go — to take a leap in the dark — trusting that it is His will and that He surely is guiding us to a new mode of selfhood.

Before this light dawns, we may have to go through much distress. Angry and impatient tears and prayers may be our lot. We feel furious with God because He allows our life to be turned upside down. God is apparently absent. He is no longer present the way He seemed to be during our functional phase of life. This absence is meant to prepare the turning to a more transcendent presence in the second period of mid-life. But we do not know that yet. He seemed so close during our years of apostolic zeal for His kingdom. Where is He now? We are grappling with His apparent absence. The path of life has turned in a way we had not expected. God's formation of us is mysterious. All we can do in a transcendence crisis is to wait in readiness for the dawn that will break upon us in the end.

Our unique spiritual life form is always emerging in and through many passing forms of life. The central means of this emergence are self-direction and self-formation. God from all eternity directs our life towards Himself in a unique way. Each emergence-crisis is a graced event. The mid-life crisis too is a divine gift, a graced opportunity for the disclosure of new directive values. When we appropriate these value directives, they become our life directives for the next period of self-formation. Only then can we begin to give form to our lives in accordance with them.

Self-formation thus means implementing value directives in our current life form. Our spiritual life unfolds through a succession of temporal self-dimensions, such as infancy, childhood, adolescence, young adulthood, first and second mid-life period, old age. Each new period of selfhood implies a new disclosure of divine directives. This disclosure leads to a crisis, a formative "dark night of the soul." It is in this way that the mystery of our divine life direction is disclosed to us over a life time. For a number of us the most decisive transcendence crisis happens in mid-life; it affects the final part of our life and may be seen as a prefiguring of death. If we do not resolve the crisis successfully, it must be dealt with later. The same is true for all previous crises.

The shift some of us are called to make in mid-life is so radical that it seems to split our life in two. Yet in the apparent discontinuity there is a continuity. This continuity is hidden in our graced lasting core self, in the nucleus of our spiritual self-direction. The lasting core self contains the mystery of our unfolding uniqueness: all the gifts and graces of former periodic selves; all the sedimented life directives that are in harmony with our divine life direction or unique divine image. During a transcendence crisis it is difficult, if not impossible, to see this hidden continuity. The gift of faith enables us to believe in this graced direction and to trust that God gives a unified meaning to our life in the midst of disruption and discontinuity. Towards the end of the crisis we may be graced with an enlightened memory: the gift to recall events and graces in our former periods of life that point to a continuity with the deeper directives disclosed to us now.

We begin to redefine success. Instead of stubbornly clinging to the definitions and understandings of a former period of life, we become ready for a transfiguration of insight. We do not root our assurance in a record of past achievements but open up to what God wills for us in the future. Faith beckons us towards the future and reminds us of the past insofar as it revealed radically God's direction for us. The crucial question is one of maintaining and enhancing a spirit of readiness. We cannot define ahead of time what our life will be like, but we can look to the future as a promise, not a threat.

Idealized Life Directives Crisis

Our transcendent self is a self of aspirations just as our functional self is a self of ambitions. Aspirations are stimulating us preconsciously long before the period of life in which they will be in the foreground of our formation efforts. For many of us that may only happen in the last half of life. Yet we are never totally without an urge to transcendence. Already early in life our innate aspirations manifest themselves in our inclination to set up ideal life directives. Our tendency to idealize is a symptom of our innate spirituality.

An ideal life directive is a wished-for event. This wish reveals a hidden awareness that we should not be satisfied with any current or periodic form of life. A vague sense of being called to an ever more transcendent life direction gives rise to an idealized vision of what we should become. The dynamism of our transcendent aspirations — as such still unknown to us — lends color, excitement and elation to our ideal directives. The functional realistic dimension of our spiritual life is still underdeveloped in our youthful years. At that time transcendent aspirations easily give rise to idealized or even "idolized" life directives, for they are not yet modulated by the sense of concrete incarnation in daily life.

Already in young adulthood in the 20's, and especially in the first phase of mid-life in the 30's, our idealized life directives undergo a redefinition. The divine call to incarnation, which is the mark of this period, combines with daily reality-testing to concretize our idealized directives. The functional period teaches us how consonant our idealized directives are, not only with the unique divine call at the heart of our selfhood but also with the divine directives speaking in the limits of our life situations. If our idealized directives are opposed to our deepest call, they cannot sufficiently sustain our self-formation. Redirection and subsequent reformation of life is necessary. This redirection should not kill our idealism but harmonize it both with the uniqueness of the divine image at our core and the demands of our daily life. For the reality of life too reveals to us the call of the Spirit. If idealized life directives are not made consonant in this way, they may simply die and with that dies our sense of aliveness and purpose.

We should give form to our lives in light of ideal life directives; they should in turn be steered by the compass of the unique divine direction which reveals itself increasingly in both inner and outer directives.

In childhood our spirituality was contaminated by a sense of magic. As children, we are easily misled by our innate but untested aspirations. We believe that we can make things come true by our wishes alone. We feel like little gods. This magical deformation of childhood spirituality is partly replaced by the incarnational aspect during the more functional periods of spiritual growth. Our ideal directives become more incarnational; they are tempered by the demands of reality. However, the dark night of the mid-life crisis may still be necessary for many of us to purify radically our idealized or idolized directives. Our spirituality is then released from its magical component; our idealized directives are reappraised. A reconciliation of the transcendent and the functional dimensions of our spiritual formation begins to take place. As a result of this reconciliation, we could possibly experience a peace and integration not known before. Idealized or idolized directives become limited, flexible ideal directives.

The special grace of the mid-life crisis is rooted in a reappraisal of idealized directives made possible by detachment. We come to understand, aspire and choose differently. This rebirth implies a certain regression, marked by a feeling of insecurity. The security of managing our own life by forcing upon it idealized or idolized directives of the past is gone. We feel a loss of control of our life. We have lost our bearings. Excessive praise or blame doew not help us. We may take praise as a reassurance that we can still realize our unrealistic life directives. Excessive blame may tell us the opposite — that we should feel guilty and ashamed because we cannot live up to our exalted self-expectations. In both instances we are still the center of our own idolized life directives. By contrast, the mid-life transcendence crisis aims at making the Holy Spirit the center and inspiration of any ideal life directives we may choose. It creates more room in us for the formative power of the pneumatic dimension of our spiritual life.

Chapter VII
CRISIS OF APPEARANCES

The spiritual self must adapt itself to its surroundings. For we live not only with ourselves but with others. This adaptation implies a guarded self-revelation — guarded, in the sense that our inmost self is vulnerable and easily misunderstood. If manifested unwisely, it might evoke disbelief, irritation, envy, ridicule and suspicion. The unreserved manifestation of our divine uniqueness may overwhelm others, hurting their independence and self-reliance. We cannot remain effective in everyday interaction if we pour out indiscriminately all we feel and think. Neither can we maintain our interiority if we let its treasures dissipate in idle talk. The inmost self loses its silent beauty when we show it off to everyone.

There must thus be a difference between who we are for ourselves and what we look like to others. Our apparent self should not reveal totally our deepest self. Each current life form we develop should maintain as one main aspect this "apparent selfhood," that is, the way we are honestly present to others, the limited but true face we show in daily life.

In other words, even our current life form should

not be delivered over to others unconditionally. The face we show should neither represent a naive surrender of our current selfhood nor a betrayal of it. It is a betrayal of our true self when our face becomes a deceitful mask or pretends attitudes foreign to us.

In the mid-life crisis we become more aware of the appearances we developed over a long history of interaction with others. Now we look at them critically. We discover, on the one hand, that some of them were dishonest. This insight is an invitation to drop or replace them. On the other hand, we realize that not all our ways of interaction were deceptive or unrealistic. Some fitted both us and the situation. In the period of functional adulthood, for example, we had to act in such a way that effective functioning would be facilitated between us and our fellow men.

If a man is involved in laboratory research, for example, he chooses wisely to show interest mainly in the common project. He does not talk about his prayer life. Yet he is not being dishonest; he would not deny his faith if questioned about it. Moreover, his dedication to research is not feigned; it manifests his motivation to foster the unfolding of mankind and world. This motivation in turn is rooted in the love of his deepest self for the Creator and His creation as well as in his wholehearted commitment to the unfolding of this creation. Briefly, there is no separation between his apparent self, current self and inmost self.

We conclude: the authentic "apparent self" is a

selective expression of only those true aspects of a person's interior life that are relevant to the situation at hand.

The mid-life crisis is evoked partly by a change in life situation. New situations demand new appearances. To change the apparent self implies a detachment from former apparent selves that have become second nature to us. This change entails the sacrifices we described earlier in relation to the mid-life crisis of detachment.

Many a middle-aged person does undergo unsettling changes. This is a period of ambivalence and uncertainty. Bored, dissatisfied, restless and hemmed in by life, some of us become filled with anxiety and apprehension. Ambiguous about the inner turmoil and desirous to hide it from ourselves and others, we may begin to wear masks that are foreign to who we are. Often this trying out of false masks is part of the process of finding appearances that fit the mid-life realities. People are aware of the masquerade of the mid-life crisis. They comment on how so-and-so is not living up to his age. Some of us may get stuck in this phase of the process. We spend the rest of our lives in tiring attempts to keep up false appearances.

The crisis of appearances begins with the awareness that our appearance does not evoke the same response as before. We dress, groom, move or speak in a youthful way. In the past it made us attractive; now people seem to find it odd, out of place, comical or pathetic.

Middle-aged men may try to ingratiate themselves

with younger women. The response of the latter may be polite reserve, pity, slight ridicule, guarded friendliness or condescending kindness.

Men and women may display the appearance of great authority in their job. But it is no longer received with the same respect. A silent resistance communicates itself.

We may now go through a phase of denial of this loss of effective appearances, often accompanied by a forced attempt to stress these appearances more than before. Finally, the failure of such willful trials leaves us no alternative but to withdraw to the center of ourselves.

We begin at this point to question our appearances from the center of our being. This questioning makes us aware of the false masks we wear. It points the way to a purification of appearances. Not all of them are deceptive. We become aware of some that are true to our deepest self but no longer true to our life situation. We cannot maintain them either. The realization that certain false and true appearances have to be abandoned is painful. A period of mourning results.

Distraught by our discovery we may go through a time of trying to live without appearances. To the outside world some of us may look sloppy, unsettled, unreliable, eccentric and out of touch with daily reality. We have forgotten that the apparent self is a necessary part of our effective spiritual life. At no age can we escape the asceticism of developing and maintaining right appearances that do not hurt others. We need to develop, therefore: a style in tune with our interiority and acceptable to our surroundings; ways of being with others that facilitate the flow of social interaction; considerate ways that protect others against the seductive power of our uniqueness and that prevent us from imposing our interiority on others. Right appearances are a fine expression of Christian love, respectful distance and true humility.

The next phase, therefore, is one of trying out new considerate ways of presence. Initially we may try on false masks because we are motivated too much by anxiety and apprehension. We want too fast to look good again. We role play furiously to hide our uncertainty. We tend to become identified with the deceptive part we play. There is a disruption between our private life and the life we pretend to live. We may identify with such pretentions, especially when they make us look better than we really are. In that case we suffer tension. We spend tremendous energy concealing from ourselves and others the aging and mellowing person we really are behind our mask of youthfulness and invulnerability. For example, we display the youthful arrogance of self-made people in need of nobody. Yet deep down we are crying out for companionship now that our outer control is waning. The more we play the indifferent role, the more we are weakened within by the stifled yearings of our heart. The result may be a sudden collapse.

For example, to his own surprise, and that of his colleagues, a good husband and father may fall in love suddenly with another woman who senses his need and voices concern. Some unexpected love relationships in middle-age between seemingly stern proud men and seductive young girls find their source in this tension between real need and make-believe appearance.

The more we discover and abandon these false masks, the more we ready ourselves for the disclosure of appropriate, considerate ways of being present to others. What are the marks of these right appearances? First of all, they must not be at odds with our inner world. Secondly, they must modulate the true manifestation of our unique divine image in accordance with our culture. Our culture has certain expectations in regard to people in the second half of life. Insofar as these expectations are justified they should be responded to in our various modes of self-appearance. The second half of mid-life exposes us to change. Our modes of self-expression should take these changes into account. Lastly, in respect and compassion our self-appearance should protect people against those aspects of our unique life form they cannot bear or cope with.

To summarize: we should shed inappropriate appearances and search for more appropriate ones. To find them we must unearth our core image and allow it to radiate its unique truth also into our apparent self. This involves shedding past modes of presence for those that are more in tune with our deepest divine image and with the new period of life we find ourselves in. The mid-life crisis offers us an opportunity to come to the heart of our unique life

form. Our appearances should flow from this heart.
Then this phase of our spiritual unfolding becomes
a graced-filled experience, enabling us to reap the
benefits of the crisis of middle-age.

Discarding past appearances serves our coming to
the truth of new ones that are more faithful both to
who we are deep down and to who we are here and
now. Detachment from past modes of presence thus
offers us one of the most creative avenues to spiritual
unfolding.

Chapter VIII

CRISIS OF DE-ACTIVATION
AND OF ULTIMATE MEANING

The crisis of de-activation demands detachment. Like other crises, it leads to a loss of balance, but it too has formative potential.

De-activation means a giving up or lessening of involvements that meant much to us before the mid-life turning point. Working through the experience of this loss prepares for the problems of retirement facing us in the future. The lessening of activity was prefigured in periods of de-activation experienced throughout life. We had to diminish our involvements in times of illness, during vacations, and perhaps in periods of solitude freely chosen or imposed on us by circumstances.

In contrast with these pauses from action, the de-activation of mid-life may be forced and lasting. We are detached, often against our will and liking, from involvements we cherished for years. They made life meaningful, gave it zest and spark, and sustained our feelings of self-worth, independence and dignity. De-activation may be accompanied by a loss of self-esteem. Lessening activity thus plays a significant part in the mid-life crisis of many people.

This same dimishment of demands enables us to disengage ourselves from certain competitive endeavors. They are no longer expected. Younger men and women take our place. The man who always cut wood for the fire, who always shoveled the snow, is gently pressed to leave these chores to his older sons. The woman who cooked the meals, set the table, and arranged festive dinners for the whole family on holidays, is assisted by daughters and in-laws, who insist that mother should take it easy. On the job, adults in their prime are asked to take charge of works aging employees used to take in stride. Similar experiences happen in social, charitable and church enterprises.

De-activation demands adjustment. It is characterized by the separation from involvements we have become accustomed to. The separation can be sudden, but more often it happens gradually. The process of redirection of our life begins when symbolic incidents make us aware of the de-activation mid-life entails. This process abates when we have achieved a satisfying redirection of our energies and a reformation of our selfhood. We adapt in the absence of chores that in the past added meaning to our life. We are not so much interested in the outer aspects of de-activation as in the inner drama that may ensue from it.

One way to cope with this loss is the way of remembrance. We should remember the past moments of de-activation God has allowed in our life: the graced duration of a holiday or quiet vacation; being at home with nothing to do; a retreat or day of recollection; a liturgical celebration; perhaps a boat or fishing trip. Sometimes these withdrawals in quiet and solitude restored our sense of self, brought us nearer to the Sacred, enabled us to feel more whole.

The difference is that we expected and cherished these moments of restoration; we knew they would be passing. What de-activation now does to many of us is to separate us lastingly from the main body of adults who are still in the period of expanding performance. We are called not so much to expand as to deepen the enterprises we can still maintain. We may also add involvements less competitive and more in keeping with our emerging capacities of wisdom and sensitivity.

Men, in particular, may shun de-activation since they often define their worth in terms of what they do: "I *am* a policeman, a teacher, a cook," or "He *is* a foreman in the mill." The extent of their responsibilities gives them a feeling of worth and usefulness.

De-activation of the middle-aged woman takes a different form. When her children have left, the scope of her activities at home is diminished. Many women today then enter or re-enter the job market or commit themselves as volunteers to social and charitable enterprises. This makes the crisis of de-activation less severe. Her outside involvements give her access to a life unknown before. Sooner or later, however, she will experience within these commitments the consequences of aging, especially when she has to compete with younger colleagues.

Single or married women who were already a part of the work force may experience, as men do, similar incidences of de-activation. The more they have defined their self-worth in terms of their functions, the more serious the crisis of de-activation will be for them.

We are describing here the average person employed in an average job. Gifted persons in creative occupations, such as writers, composers, artists, conductors and thinkers, may experience such lessening of activity much later in life, or not at all.

Not everyone feels the same resistance to de-activation. Some accept it more easily for a variety of reasons. At the root of their resignation or even relief could be a lack of involvement, a certain inertia, or a deficiency in initiative. A contemplative bent, combined with an early spiritual maturity, may enable others to welcome the benefits of de-activation. For many people, however, de-activation in mid-life contains the potential for a crisis experience.

De-activation Crisis and Culture

The crisis of de-activation is probably stronger in civilizations like ours where production is a central value. We are conditioned to make measurable achievement the index of our worthwhileness. Being less needed in the process of production evokes shame and guilt in many of us. Productivity may be inscribed in our conscience as the first commandment of the technical civilization. When less involved in performance, we feel less valued than those who prove themselves to be useful. This diminishment of production-expectancy may affect our standing in society both within our own mind and that of others.

If measurable achievement has been the focus of self-appraisal, the lessening of production-expectancy can be a cataclysmic experience. The future looks bleak without this expectancy of increasing the only capacity that seemed to give importance to our lives. Worse still, we begin to sense the end point of de-activation: total retirement from the life of production. Some of us are frightened at the prospect that the mandatory activity that structures our days will be ended in the near future and leave us lost and forlorn in the emptiness of zero-production.

De-activation means also a lessening of social status. It entails, furthermore, a diminishment of the anticipatory joy of expansion of responsibilities and the subsequent rewards of affirmation and promotion. The future looks less inviting. We may question the value of our aging presence in a society that lauds mainly achievement. De-activation threatens us with the spectre of loss of the current form of our life. It affects our expectations. We worry about the possible loss of our livelihood, our independence, and the companionship and discipline our job offers us.

Ultimate Meaning Crisis

The crisis of de-activation is interwoven with the

other crisis described so far. Together they may evoke a far deeper upheaval in many people: a crisis of ultimate meaning. The meanings that are lost or threatened may make us question the meaning of life itself.

The ultimate sense of being has to be found in our deepest self. As pragmatic people, we may not have been at home in our interiority; we became strangers to ourselves. Having to face the mystery of selfhood, we feel ill at ease. The cultural conviction that productivity is of ultimate importance has lessened our faith that the dignity of our inner divine image is paramount. We have identified ourselves with the functions we fulfill. Our value resided mainly in our effectiveness. Self and world lost much of their mystery for us. Especially in the functional phase of the mid-years, life may have seemed not much more than a process of production. The world became a pragmatic setting with no deeper meaning than that of usefulness. Now that these functional meanings are receding, life seems so empty that we feel on the verge of despair. We ask ourselves: Is that all there is to it?

We become victims of the technological civilization if we equate human dignity with functional effectiveness. Then our life *is* our effectiveness and our effectiveness *is* our reason for living. We feel that we were somebody prior to this mid-life crisis; now we do not know who or what we are. We do not feel valuable outside of our performance. We have exchanged the sacredness of who we are for what we have accomplished. Life seems useless and without meaning. We have lost touch with the aspirations within us that are a source of joy and fulfillment, that open us to the plenitude of the Transcendent, who never frustrates our expectations. Presence to the Divine quickens and refreshes life. As long as we see our worth as residing mainly in what we do, we may be tempted to bypass this mysterious core of our being. Once the mid-life crisis puts the ultimacy of performance into question, we despair. Foreseeing the decline of our productive powers, we ask ourselves what our value is if we are no more than a tool of production? To break out of the imprisonment created by such a view of life, we must turn to transcendence. Only then shall we be able to cope with the many detachments forced upon us.

The crises and detachments of the middle years compel us to reflect on our life as a whole. Each detachment imposed on us from without is an invitation to grow to detachment within. Each inner detachment is an opportunity to grow in depth, to center ourselves in the divine image at the core of our being. When we say yes to these invitations, we come to value ourselves more for who we are than for what we do. No longer do we try to deny our deprivations. Instead we search for their meaning; we make our home more at the center than at the periphery of our being. We begin to walk in the truth of who we are.

Such centering and walking in the truth becomes possible through recollection and meditation. Recollection is essential to all spiritual formation. It facilitates especially the development of the transcendent dimension of our spiritual life in the second phase of the middle years. Recollection enables us to initiate a process of inner detachment when external detachment weighs heavily upon us. Within the space created in us by recollection, we will be able to come to terms with deprivation experiences and to center ourselves in the Divine.

Chapter IX

RECOLLECTION AND MID-LIFE MEDITATION

At the moment of recollection, we distance ourselves from our preoccupations; we draw near to the mystery of our ground. Recollection is a pause in the stream of experiences that threaten to engulf us during a transcendence crisis. It creates a point of rest from which we can gain a better view of what is happening to us. We enter into an inner, sacred domain. We silence the noise of life and hear the whisper of the psalmist: Be still and know that I am God. In this stillness before Him, we allow our experiences to speak to us, to disclose their deeper meaning.

Recollection is a time to be alone, away from the feelings that drain or agitate us. Only by rising beyond the whirl of feelings can we master them. We cease temporarily from expending energy in reaction to people, events and things that arouse agitation.

Such moments of recollection are essential to formation. They are especially meaningful in the second phase of mid-life. For the first time we may feel attuned to the inner form or image of the

Transcendent in us. Inner changes take place that diminish the need for constant socializing. The Divine Director of universe and humanity calls us to recollection.

Recollection is a condition for meditation on God, self, life and death, on past, present and future. It becomes possible only when it is not confused with introspection. It should give rise to a self-presence that is transcendent. We are called to be present to our life not as if it were an isolated thing to be dissected but as a mystery rooted in an all-embracing, caring presence. This gentle self-presence attunes us to a mysterious love that already enfolds us and gives meaning to our life and its crises of transition.

Formative graces turn us inward with advancing age. We experience a change of heart. We are more inclined to re-collect our energies, spread out as they are in a secular world, and to direct them to the inward meaning of self and situation. The need for recollection creates the greatest opportunity to unveil our divine image. We turn away from the fads that dominate society, from the slogans and opinions others try to catch us with. We become interested in contemplation and the creative functioning that may flow from it. We center in the heart, in the divine mystery that carries and forms us and our world constantly. We feel refreshed and renewed as we nurture the companionship of the Trinity and begin to treasure moments of solitude. Departure from mere functional concerns may be difficult at first; it is like losing familiar surroundings, but in the midst of this aridity we may touch the mystery that dwells in us and our world.

As long as the practical dimension of our spiritual life prevails, the aspiration for recollection lies dormant and untapped. Deprivation experiences awaken this aspiration. In recollection we may be led to center ourselves in the Divine as the foundational meaning of life and world.

Recollection also has as its purpose to sustain the inner detachment that must be our response to the outer detachments imposed on us in a transcendence crisis. Inner detachment is a process, not an abrupt happening like the imposed detachment that may give rise to it. It implies a gradual acceptance of the suffering a transcendence crisis entails. We bid a gentle farewell to the gifts God intended for the former periods of life. This growth in acceptance, this leave-taking in love, enable us to integrate detachments in our life. We touch in a deeper, interior way the formative meaning of mid-life deprivations.

Recollection can be confused not only with introspection but also with a flight from reality and a forsaking of life. Giving up functionalism should not mean to give up functioning. Functioning as well as we can remains an essential dimension of the Christian spiritual life, also in the second phase of the mid-years. Christian spirituality is incarnational; we cannot incarnate if we flee from creative functioning. What we must relinquish are certain modes and intensities of functioning. What we must abandon above all is functionalism — the domination of our life by values of functioning as if they were ultimate. Our functioning must become the disciple of the transcendent experiences gained in recollection and meditation.

In recollection we realize how a transcendence crisis has broken the sense of continuity in our life. As we meditate, we try to find a deeper spiritual sense in what is happening to us. We begin to see how the present and the future looming ahead can be re-conciled with the losses of the past. In the light of transcendent meaning, a healing sense of coherence re-asserts itself. Periodic recollections enable us to recoup our inner resources, to renew ourselves in faith, hope and love. This strengthening of inner forces encourages us not to escape the pain of detachment by denial or repression but to experience it as a challenge to open up to a higher dimension of spiritual formation.

Recollection in and by itself is not enough. We should, therefore, meditate on what happens to us; we should prayerfully bend back on what God allows to be in this phase of our spiritual formation.

There are many ways and subjects of meditation, but basically it is a prayerful presence to a mystery of faith or to our life as envisioned in faith. Faith reflection emerges in times of transition when detach-ments disturb our peace. Its aim is to disclose God's unique direction for the remainder of our life.

The later mid-years may begin for many of us with this faith reflection. It moves us to transform the modes of presence that dominated our spiritual life

prior to this turning point. Prayerful meditation leads
to a deepening of interiority. We no longer trust that
the forces that have carried us until now will grant us
fulfillment. We discover an unknown and secret life
that resides within us and our world, always ready to
transform us. For the Christian the mystery of God's
forming love is found from eternity in a community of
three divine persons; this same love calls us in Jesus
to share in that ongoing divine formation in the image
of the Trinity: one in community with others yet
unique as persons.

ʹThe last half of life offers many people their best
opportunity to be formed as persons within a
community. In mid-life meditation we gain distance
from roles that we mistook for our true identity.
Disclosed to us is the transcendent mystery that we
are co-authors with God, graced centers of free
initiative, no longer the slaves of socially imposed
models.

Up to this turning point, life for some was a collection of social niceties, functional duties, countless
distractions. They lived in a state of confusion that
obscured the perception of their divine life call. Mid-
life meditation helps the person correct his course. He
can begin to take possession of himself as called
forth by God, who knows his true name.

Recollection gave birth to this faith reflection,
which deepens in solitude. In the sanctuary of
inwardness we face our iltimate loneliness. Initially
it gives rise to anxiety; for we are being elevated
beyond the ties that supported us until this moment.

Meditation reaches its culmination when God infuses the strength to distance ourselves from the supports that consoled and carried us to this turning point. We are dispossessed of people, things and relationships we thought would be lasting. In the solitude of recollection, we meet our deeper divine image that rests in God. We are called by Him out of a functional society that cannot satisfy our inmost longings. As we become less distracted and absorbed by superficial excitements, as we find ourselves in solitude, paradoxically we discover the true sense of community.

Mid-life meditation begins when we ask such questions as: What does my life mean in the eyes of God? What is He trying to tell me by this detachment? Where does He want me to go? I linger on the brink of divine depths, free to choose the life of the Spirit or to fling myself back into the distractions of a mere social-functional life. The divine invitation is given. I can accept or refuse. In making my choice I choose my life direction — the direction that will give form to the remainder of my journey. I may decide not to transcend my past, to escape the whisper of the Spirit, to deny the divine invitation. I may deprive myself of the wisdom and love that is meant to flow from prayerful presence to this painful situation or I may turn to the mystery of the divine direction of my life.

How long the period of mid-life meditation will last depends on the grace of God as well as on the past history and present turmoil of each person. It is not only a question of intellectual understanding and acceptance of the mid-life predicament. It is fore-most a question of the heart. The mid-life meditation must move our heart, not only our mind. Our innermost center must be touched. The turn to transcendence in an interior event. The crisis of detachment is only the outer stimulant to the heart-felt transition I am invited to make. I must allow myself inwardly to be drowned, as it were, in the divine invitation that hides in detachment.

Initially the mind may prevail, but gradually, as the mid-life meditation deepens, I begin to under-stand what God means by allowing this crisis in my life. I begin to grasp where He is leading me though I may not be able as yet to wholeheartedly embrace my destiny. My heart resists these painful depriva-tions. Meditation is still permeated by spasms of pain about detachments not yet accepted. I feel compelled to go over them again and again; in the tortuous process of coming to terms with grief, I may slip back in anger and frustration, in numbness and despair. Only slowly may I begin to sense that I am asked to let go of more than the powers, pleasures and successes that dominate me. I am asked to let go of my self, to surrender to His direction, to allow Him to transform me inwardly and to ready me for the mystery of the rest of my life.

Chapter X

THE WORLD AS THE HOUSE OF GOD

When we have worked through the mid-life crisis in recollection and meditation, our spiritual life, that seemed dead and buried, erupts again with new intensity. We experience a fresh surge of spirituality. It absorbs the best of the past into the transcendent turn our life has taken; it transforms the world into the House of God. The labor of the mid-life crisis is over; the struggle to be reborn is won. We have faced the detachments God allowed in our life and received the grace to open up to Him and His presence in creation.

Gradually, perhaps even unawares, we feel a new form of life emerging, and with it a new world. Sometimes gently, sometimes intensely, something is forming within. We begin to experience the inner dynamic of transformation. Where once we felt barren, we feel the stirring of life. Initially, it is a dark wordless process, hesitant and vulnerable, a reaping of the first benefits of graced suffering and of transfigured vision. Cut free from the idealisms of the past, we open up to a more realistic life, which accepts that fullness is at the same time emptiness;

that satisfaction is clouded by displeasure; that security is pervaded by uncertainty; and yet that all of this is ultimately meaningful in a world which is experienced now as God's mysterious dwelling place.

The unimportance, irrelevancy and even meaninglessness of many of our functionalistic views of self and world are revealed to us. The radical turn to transcendence begins to restore the wholeness of our spiritual life and the transcendent meaning of the world which may have been lost during the crisis or perhaps never had emerged for us. Slowly joy, peace, and serenity enter our later years. They enable us to return to daily life with a deeper sense of presence to the transcendent in creation.

Our indestructible longing for transcendent meaning is finally finding its object. We do not feel useless because we are not as useful as before. We experience a homecoming in the all-encompassing mystery of the House of God in which we are immersed.

As Guardini describes it:

> Existence now takes on the character, we might say, of a still-life in Cezanne. There is a table. Upon the table, a plate. Upon the plate, some apples. Nothing else. Everything is there, clear and evident. Nothing left to ask nor to answer. And yet, mystery everywhere. There is more in these things than meets the eye: more than the simple individuality of each thing. You begin to think that the mystery is in the clarity . . . It might even be that mystery is the very stuff of being: things, events, everything that hap-

pens, and which we call "life" . . . a mystery which you feel is a signal that reality itself sends out to us. (Romano Guardini "The Stages of Life and Philosophy," *Philosophy Today,* 1:2-4 (June, 1957), 78-79).

After the turn to transcendence we no longer deny such manifestations of transcendent presence. Becoming more at home with mystery, we welcome such invasions of lucidity.

This awareness is comparable to the mellow light of the autumn of life; it holds us up when we surrender to it; it redeems us from mere functionality; it enables us to work and care in a playful way. The liberated person has transcended the wearisome, greedy, tense, panicky approach to life that marked him before the turn to transcendence. Functionalism is never totally absent. It lurks in the depths of our past life as an ever present threat. At any time it might reappear and ensnare us again. The difference is that we know now experientially of the Transcendent Love always there to restore us to the vision of the world as the divine dwelling place. No matter how much our life becomes muddled we know we can return to Him in trust and confidence. The crisis has opened a window into the world which will never be shut again.

Once we have touched the Heart of Reality and felt its healing presence, the memory lingers on in us and keeps calling us back. When we live in the shelter of this luminous presence, our days become simplified. This shelter is not the isolating prison of the functional ego. Paradoxically, the whole world is the shelter of the transcendent self — not the world as projected by the manipulating ego but the world that reveals itself as "Domus Dei," the House of God, the sanctuary of His presence.

The same world that distracts, scatters and tempts the functionalistic person heals, illumines and forms graciously the transcendent one. The enlightenment that follows the mid-life struggle does not absolve us from recollection and meditation. No longer is mid-life meditation a prayerful consideration of the crisis of life; it becomes a silent presence to the Presence, a simple attentiveness to be cultivated during the day in many "mini-pauses."

Each person is different and unique. We all have to find our own ways of attentiveness, our own mode of maintaining a sense of the Transcendent in daily strivings, of dwelling in our surroundings reverently as in the House of God. We should not be surprised to find ourselves struggling again with the old custom to trim down the dignity of each person, event and thing to their usefulness only. It takes time and patience before the turn to transcendence in the core of our being heals the whole of us. This purification may not be achieved at the end of life. Then the gift of final purification awaits us in a last period of purification, a mysterious crisis of the soul that far surpasses the transcendence crises in life. This other crisis, because of its purifying, forming power, has traditionally been called purgatory. The unique life form meant for us from eternity will there become ours in its fullness.

Insofar as the world reveals itself as Domus Dei,

the House of God, a transcendent home, we will live a more responsive and reflective presence to its nature, people and happenings. The turn to transcendence, far from taking us out of the world, brings us back to it in a whole new way. To be sure, we may slip back into a life of forgetfulness but an inner restlessness calls us to return to the Transcendent. Sufferings and disappointments, detachments and deprivations will not cease, but now we allow them to speak their truth to us. They become opportunities to make a home for ourselves and others in the world as the House of God.

Suffering stirs that complacency that would settle and dull our lives. For this reason the process of ongoing formation remains necessary after the turn to transcendence. Its greatest enemy is complacency because it prevents the release of our newly found divine life form into every dimension of our personality and of our surroundings.

Mid-life detachment made us aware that fulfillment is not found in clinging to all we can grasp. Filling ourselves in this way led to clutter and confusion. In the phase of acquisition and expansion, we became bloated with everything possible. During this crisis things were taken away we thought we could not do without. Then we discovered that not only could we live without them, but we could be much more at ease that way. We realized that the second half of life is a way of letting go rather than of taking in, a period of simplicity rather than complexity. Instead of being possessed by things, we became present to their symbolic meanings, their silent power of transformation.

The second half of life is a time of release of excessive control, of calming down the frenzied search for information. We allow wisdom to grow ahead of information and divine direction to take over manipulation. We let go of what we most prize, develop and rely upon: control of our lives and our world. The detachments we suffered are an invitation to cultivate a gentle attentiveness to meanings that go beyond manipulation. The mid-life crisis has thrown us onto a strange shore which owes nothing to the expertise we gained during the first phase of the middle years.

During this crisis the purging of the clutter of life was an almost violent experience. We did not choose it; it chose us. Our acceptance led to a solution of the crisis, but it did not end the way of purgation. The purge will go on at a more gradual pace. We are ready to cope with new detachments in a relaxed and gentle way. Even after death, a final period of formation may be needed. As noted earlier, the crisis of purgatory will bring to perfection what these earthly transcendence crises began.

The mid-life crisis — like other transcendence crises — thus redirects and deepens our course. We need the remainder of life itself to implement that direction, to allow it to pervade all dimensions of our personality. This graced direction will slowly melt the resistance it meets; it will reduce the fragmentation and frantic clutch of our functional mind.

It does not destroy the functional dimension of the spiritual life, but it elevates, modulates and purifies its incarnating power.

Together with wisdom we are called to cultivate compassion. The functional phase of spiritual growth was often tinged by the coldness of efficiency. There was a tendency to judge people mainly by their usefulness. In an incarnational spirituality the criterion of usefulness cannot be relinquished. But it will no longer be the judge of the ultimate value of a human being. Our sharing in God's own compassion mellows our judgment. The wisdom of middle-age sees deeper than our organizational mind. This wisdom discloses the dignity of people even when they have to be relieved by us of tasks they are not faithful to because of lack of skill or dedication.

Middle-age wisdom appraises and upholds the diligence, skill, discipline and sustained dedication which the transfiguration of the earth as the House of God demands of all of us. It curbs the influence of those whose negativity threatens the divine project. After the mid-life crisis we no longer condemn ultimately the neurotic or sentimental person, the lax and lazy one. Only God knows how innocent or guilty they are of niggardly counting the hours, of their lack of zeal, discipline, and precision. He alone knows their past history, sufferings, problems and warped feelings. Yet also love for the many who are harmed by their failings pervades our hearts. We feel obligated in conscience to relieve the charming but unconcerned of positions they corrupt by neglect or self-serving manipulation, but we relieve them respectfully. We show them that we regret that they do not fit as well as others could into this specific position. Presence to the transforming operation of God in this world gives the middle-aged leader the courage to engage in this sacred duty of removal of the incompetent and unconcerned. He does his duty in spite of misunderstanding, threat, hostility and anger. Because he serves the direction of God, he fears less losing his popularity with people.

Our Life of Prayer after the Crisis

St. Paul asks us to pray always. In the functional phase of our spiritual life that may have seemed impossible; yet we know from the lives of many people in the second half of life that prayer can become a way of life, something that stays with us no matter what we are doing or thinking. How can the transcendent phase of life help us to pray that way?

The turn to transcendence makes us aware that we can only learn to pray by praying. Our functional life relied much on information, method and technique. We were inclined to restrict ourselves to reading books about prayer in the same way as we read do-it-yourself books about loving, child rearing and how to make friends and foster relations. At times we got so wrapped up in words about prayer that we forgot to pray. The turn to transcendence made us aware that without the experience itself of prayer the words do not mean much to us. We realize that not everything about prayer can be put into words. Even the words of the scriptures will mean something only when we try to live and experience them. After the forgetfulness of the functional years, we want to learn to pray again.

There are many ways in which the mid-life person tries to keep in contact with the Transcendent he rediscovered at the turn of life not only in himself but also in the world as God's dwelling place. Each way is limited. But we may learn from all of them as long as we really try them out. First we try to talk to God. That is a good beginning. But after some time we will find out that it does not go far enough. We feel that this talking keeps the Transcendent too much at a distance. We want to experience Him as near to us, as truly within us and within His world as in His own house. We want an answer. We like to see prayer as a conversation with the Omnipresent.

That is a good intuition, for the Transcendent really responds to us. The difficulty is we cannot hear Him as we can hear the voice of a friend. After we turn to the Transcendent, it still takes time to hear His voice both in the intimacy of our heart and in His world. We must bring Him nearer to us. Therefore, we may begin to think more about Christ, the saints, the mysteries of our faith, God's indwelling in His Creation. We think about ourselves and others and what happens around us. The turn to transcendence inclines us to think too about God and His words and His presence in all that is. That kind of prayer is called meditation. It is less difficult to learn for those who came through the mid-life crisis. The crisis made us meditate often, though not always on our faith. We meditated on opportunities lost, on the illness or death of a parent, friend, colleague or child, on physical decline and fatigue, on the meaning of the world. Meditation becomes prayerful when we begin also to think about God and His love and His presence in this world.

This kind of prayer deepens the transcendent interest that has been awakened in us at the end of our crisis. It is a great step forwards. Yet after a period of time spent in this meditation we may feel a deeper desire. We become aware that we see the Transcendent still too much as outside ourselves and outside of His creation, that we get caught in speculations and games of the mind that were typical of the functional phase of our spiritual life. To bring Him more within our life and surroundings, we let God enter into our reflections on self and world. Aging, we feel more the need to muse about what happens to us during the day and what happens to the world and its history.

The older we become the more we engage in such reflections. We sit down quietly and, while the events of the day flow through our mind, we keep our heart turned to Him. Doing so we develop a personal relationship with the Transcendent; we allow Him to become more and more at home in our lives and in our world. It is like a human relationship. It keeps growing through talking and being with another. It begins with talk, conversation, then understanding each other more and more, becoming at home with each other; finally, there emerges something we cannot really describe in words; it is too transcendent for that. We call it love. If love grows deeper, we need less words; we can be silent together and enjoy being close: at home with the Divine in and around us.

At this stage of our transcendent life, we may imagine ourselves in close relationship to Jesus as we know Him from the gospels. This contact may satisfy us for a long period of time. Growing older, however, God may call us gradually to an even more transcendent prayer that is less tangible. Initially we may be tempted to cling to the imaginative way of praying, which proved so helpful during the first months or years after our turn to transcendence. But gradually we let go of these images and feelings. We begin to live in the presence of the God who is a mystery that cannot be imagined or felt. This is the beginning of always praying as St. Paul recommends. We try in a relaxed way to become aware of the presence of the Transcendent all the time we are awake. We need the grace of quiet concentration and perseverance to develop this habit. We become truly at home in the House of God.

Gradually awareness of transcendent presence becomes an underlying theme of the last half of life, an undercurrent that never leaves us totally. This silent orientation towards the Transcendent is more spiritual and less bound to images than the former kinds of prayer.

The transcendent knowing of God in prayer is not

the functional knowing characteristic of the first phase of the mid-life years. It is making room in myself for an experience of His loving presence deep within me and all around me. This life of transcendent presence in prayer will not always be easy. There will be periods of aridity in which praying seems dull and empty. But the autumn of life knows also periods of love and peace, indescribable in their beauty.

To grow in prayerful transcendence, we must try in inner quiet to live continually in the faith that the Transcendent is alive and at work deep within us and within our world. We must be ready to give some time and effort to prayer daily, to bear with boredom until the Transcendent in His own good time breaks through in us.

Remaining in the presence of the Transcendent is the condition of always praying. There must be a way of keeping in touch with Him that is open to each of us in the mellowing years of growing older gracefully. How do we keep in touch with our family, our best friends, our beloved, our children and grandchildren now that we are less functionally involved in their lives? We do it in many ways: visits, postcards, letters, a birthday or Christmas gift, telephone conversations, pictures, remembrances. It is necessary that we do this often enough to keep the relationship alive.

Remaining in the presence of the Transcendent happens somewhat in the same way. Jesus Himself gave the example. The core of His life was keeping in touch with the Father. Time and again He created a moment of stillness in His life to be alone with God. These moments flowed over into the rest of His life.

He was always abiding with His Father. This presence was nourished by the manifestations of the Father's indwelling in the world and by the words of the scriptures He had meditated upon since His youth. To follow the way of Jesus is to create moments of stillness in our lives; to pay attention to God's world and to God's words as they come to us in our reading of the scriptures, the spiritual masters and in the words of the liturgy.

As soon as a word strikes us, fills us with peace, we should treasure it in our hearts like Mary did the words of Jesus. We should take it with us in our daily life, come back to it again and again. It is our mid-life point of contact with the One who remains in us; it is our way of remaining in Him.

The more reflective stance of the middle years may encourage us to make a collection of words and sentences that have proven to be of help in this regard. They can serve as bridges between our mid-life musings and the Lord within us. At any lost moment during the day, we may try to remember the words we have chosen as signposts of our presence to the Transcendent in self and world. We should not try to reason about such words as we were inclined to do during the functional phase before the mid-life crisis. We should allow them to penetrate our last half of life as fragrant oil saturates a dried-up sponge.

Neither should we be forceful in our attention as we were when driven by the willfulness of the phase of mastery and control. The transcendent phase of life should be marked by a waiting in patience, ready to receive the imprint of the holy word in the depth of our soul, yet also ready to bear with the absence of consolation.

What counts is a steady returning to the words of the Lord, of His Church, of His apostles, saints and spiritual masters and to experience self and world in their light. This return will keep our middle years oriented towards Him. We are truly abiding in Him even if we do not feel the effects of His remaining in us. In His own good time He may grant us moments of the experience of His presence. They may be fleeting but precious. Growing older we may receive the grace St. Paul speaks about: the grace to pray always, to be always at home in the world as the House of God.

Chapter XI
REPENTANCE IN MID-LIFE SPIRITUALITY

At all times a mysterious call pleads with us to realize the divine form of life meant for us from eternity. The mid-life crisis makes us more available to this summons; sensitivity to its sound deepens in the autumn of life. The call announces itself in two ways. It inspires us to go forward, to disclose the path ahead; it also invites us to bend backwards over the route travelled so far; it awakens us to past detours; it makes us repent of opportunities neglected, of directives disobeyed.

Repentance is an invitation to acknowledge the counterfeit forms we allowed to proliferate in our lives; it enables the form of God in which we are created to emerge more fully towards the end of our life. Less absorbed in conquest, we are able to profit more from reflections on failures that misdirected our journey. Relaxed repentance should be a faithful companion during the later part of our pilgrimage. If we do not heed its call, we have not yet reached or solved the mid-life crisis in a transcendent way.

The mere functional person may believe naively that he is doing fine, that he moves victoriously in the right direction. He steels his mind against repentance; he resents remorse as a reduction of his focus on performance. The mid-life crisis reveals to us the healing power of penance, the reconciliation that repentance provides. We no longer defy the invitation to remorse or slink away from failures we denied in the past. We take an honest look at our wanderings through life. Before eternity closes in on us, repentance calls us back from the wrong paths we took. It reminds us of how often pursuit of achievement led us astray, how we pressed on in wrong directions.

The call forward does not fall silent. It too is heeded, for exclusive remorse would sour and exhaust us. Repentance in this sense is one of the sources of wisdom in advancing age. Only by openness to both communications of the divine life direction (backward and forward) can we find the healing that is the special grace of a life that comes to maturity.

The repentant heart may seem like a needless burden that slows the traveller down. In a way it does. But what is lost in speed is regained in depth of experience and sureness of direction. During the first half of life our spiritual journey seems faster because we do not count the hours lost in losing our way and retracing our path. Now we seem to advance slowly. Yet awareness of where we went astray guards us against repeating our errors. In the end we arrive earlier than we would have if we had neglected the message of remorse. We are like the driver who cautiously follows a map drawn from former experience. He stops repeatedly, looks at his map, studies the road signs and remembers where he went wrong in the past. An eager adventurer may pass him by cheerfully, yet arrive later at his destiny. Without a map and the wisdom of past experience he got lost along deceptive roads. A similar difference applies to the quality of our experience. The eager driver with only the end-point in mind pays little attention to what the surroundings have to offer. The person who drives calmly is more aware of the scenery that unrolls along the highway. He grows in experiences of things that passed by unnoticed when our chief concern is speed and efficiency.

The guide of remorse makes confession dear to us in our advancing years. The sacrament of reconciliation suits the age of reconciliation. The mid-life crisis opened us to the reality of the final moment of life. We may have felt vigorous before the crisis; death still seemed a long way off. Now we know it will come as surely as it came to many around us. The agitation of guilt reminds us that we should be on the path of wholeness before life ends. Perfect wholeness will never be ours in this life, but we are invited to intentional wholeness. It could be described as being on the way to wholeness, the wholeness of good will. This wholeness is attained by acknowledgment of our guilt, by confession and forgiveness.

The alternative to repentance is repression. Repression denies our sinfulness and failures. It sets up a division in our personality. Our energy is absorbed in defense and denial of what is a real part of us. Our repressed dark side keeps poisoning our life like the hidden fall-out of a nuclear explosion. No wholeness is possible. The older and weaker we grow the more pernicious this taxation of our waning energies by repressed guilt becomes. If in old age the guilt suddenly breaks through we may panic. We did not learn in time to live with guilt; we remained novices in the art of reconciliation. By not following the call of repentance, we wasted a great deal of time; by believing that we still had a long life before us we courted self-deceit.

Mid-age remorse educates us to the right use of time; it liberates us from the shaky presumption that a long life stretches before us. The Holy Spirit awakens remorse in us so that we may begin to understand life in a wholly different way.

Before this time, we may have felt repentant, but its effects did not last. Missing was the inward and lasting remorse the turn to transcendence would create in us later. Age makes us more sober and lonely inwardly. We face alone the great Alone. We realize we have to render an account of what we did with our life. Life begins to look differently in the light of approaching eternity.

Ripe repentance is tempered by faith, hope and love. It fills us with peace not sadness; it sets us free for surrender to God's forgiving love; it moves us from repression to reconciliation. Eternal love respects our frailty; it does not wish guilt to over-whelm us suddenly. We are invited to grow into repentance gradually. If guilt begins to excite our imagination excessively, God wants us to pause, to withdraw for a moment from the pangs of conscience. Formative guilt is meant to heal, not to confuse or destroy. Formative repentance is not the same as a passing excessive experience of contrition. Passionate contrition may shock us momentarily, but rarely does it develop into the patient power of ongoing formation that shapes and pacifies the last half of life.

Instead of strengthening and comforting us, violent incidents of remorse strain and weaken our spiritual life. They are filled with impatience. A desperate convulsive sorrow is too selfish and sensual to become the blessing of repentance. It lacks true inwardness. The complacent flow of vital-functional life before the crisis may have been punctured at times by this rage of violent guilt. Underlying this violence was an impatient desire to get it over with all at once. We wanted to hurry back to effective performance, not to be delayed by lasting repentance. By intense and fiery contrition we hoped to effect a final purification after which we would sink back in forgetfulness of the dark side of our selfhood.

In that period of our formation, there was something in the experience of guilt that terrified us. We wanted to eradicate it all at once, to avoid despair, to go on with the business of living. Our involvement in functional life accommodated this wish. Now this evasion from inner turmoil is less available; life is less busy. Thrown back on ourselves, we experience the blessed impossibility of escaping repentance. The memory of guilt begins to shout at us with a compelling voice. No other way is left for us than to resign ourselves to the forgiveness of God, growing in surrender and humility. Remorse becomes a daily, silent power of union with the divine image deep within us. We are deepened daily through the transformation of our heart by loving sorrow. We are reminded of the transformation of Peter, Mary Magdalene, Augustine and countless other saints through their life-long repentance in love. They become the patron saints of the middle years of life.

The mature repentance of the middle years is no longer impatient, anxious, restless or agonizing. It is filled with a sorrow that is mellow and deep, felt as a blessing, yet at the same time strong and powerful. Guilt is never forgotten but treasured before God. It makes us at one with ourself — an at-one-ness no longer broken by denial of our vulnerability. Mature repentance does not dwell on sordid details of the past but keeps us present to our woundedness; it makes us feel at peace in this presence. The disposition of peaceful repentance makes the middle-aged person most acceptable to God.

In the busyness of the functional life we frantically started many enterprises, tried to accomplish a thousand things at once and were often not totally with any one of them. We led a dispersed and divided life. At-one-ness with self at the time of functional formation was seldom experienced. We were not usually recollected. The middle years after the crisis offer by contrast occasions of stillness. In silence we feel emerging what lies hidden in the depths of our life, the unspeakable mystery of God's presence and the equally unspeakable remorse for our infidelity.

In the functional phase of mid-life we were often too inundated in projects to notice His presence. The mid-life crisis made us stand still; we discovered the Mystery. We began to listen attentively. It captured us. In its light we could not miss our infidelity, but the ongoing sorrow of remorse relieved our grief about being unfaithful; it convinced us anew of the Love that forms our life so tenderly.

Transcendence and Self-Denial

In the functional phase of our spiritual life, we may have approached penance from the wrong perspective. We thought of it as an achievement. We were aggressive in our self-affliction; it was filled with subtle, spiritual pride. After the turn to transcendence we experience penance more readily as a turning to God. We see it from the transcendent angle. We feel spurred on to gather our whole past and present together, to turn away from our preoccupation with self-perfection and towards God.

The turn to transcendence is a conversion from a lower form of spiritual life to a more transcendent, less selfish way of spirituality. We trust less our own power for spiritual growth and turn more to grace for liberation. We stretch out towards the love that casts out fear. During the functional formation period, our fear of failure was nourished in part by the ambition to make something of our life that would please God and other people. Failure led often to depression. Now we fear not so much looking bad in our own eyes and those of others as we fear offending God's love. We pray that the Transcendent will take over our life in its final decades, that He will purify it by His compassion even if we do not see conspicuous signs of improvement. Carried by this faith, we feel spurred on to heal our past by accepting penance for our failings.

When our spiritual formation was dominated by vital and functional strivings, we were achievement-oriented also in our spiritual life. We set great store by external practices of expiation. Soon we became tired out by such performances. We forgot about penance altogether. The turn to transcendence after the mid-life crisis was also a turning inward. It gave birth to the awareness that first of all our interiority should be cultivated. Penance should be an inner disposition rather than a collection of striking expiations. Compunction should be a movement of the loving heart, leading to self-denial. The forms this denial assumes should not be dictated by the functional ego but by grace and the wisdom the Spirit grants in advancing age.

The essence of transcendent penance is the denial of the dominance of the vital and functional self. This denial must incarnate itself in concrete penances. No one can spell out in advance what these incarnations of the transcendent attitude will be. It depends on the unexpected ways in which the vital-functional self may try to reassert its dominance in each of us during the last half of life. It depends most of all on the unique invitations of grace that come our way.

Mid-life penance is marked by the surrender of our whole self to the divine life direction. It is acceptance and endurance of the increasing detachments aging entails. Humility and charity are the sources of penance. Before the mid-life crisis these sources might have been polluted by the ambition of the ego to steel our will to toughness, to make us effective, impressive and austere in the service of God. The detachments that accompany aging do little to enhance such pride and self-reliance. A prayerful readiness for them implies that we keep ourselves in relaxed flexibility. We rely upon the grace of the divine life direction as it manifests itself from day to day. It is more an attitude of waiting than of bracing ourselves to execute sternly divine directions.

To mold ourselves rigidly was a real temptation in the functional phase of striving after perfection. We tried to harden ourselves by holy regimentation. The turn to transcendence invites us to become more and more supple, to loosen ourselves from rigid resolutions and planned mortifications, to keep open to any directive the Spirit may give. In short, we put ourselves wholly in the hands of God.

During the functional phase we hand over aspects of life; advancing age inspires us to hand over our life as a whole. The more we grow in the disposition that God may do with us as He wishes, the more we are ready for the disappointments and debilitations the later years have in store for us. There is no fuller penance than this. We will still suffer, but we will not exhaust ourselves in fighting the trials of aging that nobody can escape. What keeps us humble at this stage of life is that we ourselves do not select what to give to God. We yield ourselves up to any purification aging entails. We have no choice in the matter and, if we surrender in faith and love, He will supply the grace necessary to relinquish without bitterness what aging takes away. The disposition of surrender to divine directives is not our doing. It is Jesus' disposition in us, a gift of grace.

The pain of aging is not spectacular, picturesque or dramatic. The sufferings endured in functional performance for the Lord when we were younger may have been dramatic. They had the glamour of "battles for the Kingdom." They may have impressed family, friends and collaborators as almost heroic. They fired our imagination while filling our hearts with complacency. The countless irritations that accompany aging do not invite the applause of others. Neither do they excite anyone's imagination. They are a plain and prosaic burden that makes us share the Passion of Jesus. We are less exposed now to those beguiling phantasies that defeated the work of self-denial during the first half of life. We become more perceptive of the silent work of grace.

Finding its source and end in grace, the penance of aging becomes a prayer of praise. Prayer and penance are related; they are daily expressions of the deeper presence to the Transcendent we were invited to when life took its decisive turn.

Aging gives us the uneasy feeling that we are dying a litle. The spirit of penance restores in us a new sense of spiritual life. *"So then my brothers, there is no necessity for us to obey our unspiritual selves or to live unspiritual lives. If you do live in that way, you are doomed to die; but if by the spirit you put an end to the misdeeds of the body you will live."* (Rm. 8:12-13) *"Sharing his [Christ's] sufferings so as to share his glory."* (Rm. 8:17) *"I live now not with my own life but with the life of Christ who lives in me."* (Ga. 2:20) *"So do you also reckon that you are dead to sin, but alive unto God in Christ Jesus our Lord."* (Rm. 6:2) (cf. I P. 2:21-24 and Rm. 6:3-5).

The grief of growing older makes us sense the appeal of our Lord: *"I looked for one that would grieve together with me, but there was none."* (Ps. 95:3) Grieving with Him we lay aside the dominance of our old selfhood and take on our deeper transcendent self in Christ. *"You must put aside your old self, which gets corrupted by following illusory desires. Your mind must be renewed by a spiritual revolution so that you can put on the new self that has been created in God's way, in the goodness and holiness of the truth."* (Ep. 4:22-24).

Chapter XII

CREATIVITY AND TRANSCENDENCE

The functional dimension of the spiritual life serves the incarnation of our spirituality in self and world. Inspiration and incarnation are essential poles of the Christian life. The functional dimension should not be neglected after the turn to transcendence. It remains as essential as ever, only its mode of action changes. First of all, functionality is no longer the master but the servant of the transcendent dimension of the spiritual life. Secondly, the decline in vital energy and social opportunities stems the unbridled expansion of functional control and power. Finally, our functionality deepens and becomes more an instrument of our creativity during the last half of life.

The detachments the mid-life crisis effected in our life make us more free for creative thinking. Such reflection gives birth to innovative ideas. Creativity can enrich our middle years immensely. These are the years to broaden and enhance our creative gifts. The object of creative thought may be as simple as a change in life style or as profound as trying another position or occupation, a second career. It is important to follow our idea of change through within reason, making a real effort to see if it works. Any time we make even a small move forward, we grow in confidence and competence. Being less involved in functional competition, we can give more time to finding creative solutions to the problems we see around us.

Overinvolvement in a job or project blinds us to alternative solutions. The detachment of middle age liberates us for new perspectives. It forces creative potentials upwards; it opens fresh vistas. We may redress shortcomings in our lives we did not know existed. For many people the functional phase of life was a barren era for creativity. Creativity does not flourish when the atmosphere is unfavorable. Enlisted in some highly organized enterprise, many of us are forced to give all our time and energy to the complex routines of the job. Little time is left to be alone, to come in touch with our inner self. Constant focus on performance limits the opportunities for expansion of inner resources. We do not have time to muse, dream, reflect and meditate. We do not allow our mind to move freely in any direction. We are not really open to any new thought or idea brought to our attention.

Conversion from the dominance of the functional self to the freedom of a transcendent life means liberty. Renunciation of vital and functional fixations sets us free for creation. Freedom, creativity, peace and penance go together. Renunciation does not stifle creativity but emancipates it. Our mind expands when we are wholly submitted to the Spirit. Our creative powers are cramped or distorted when harnassed exclusively to social functions. The turn to transcendence generates vitality. We want to function for God in this world but our functioning is now made flexible and creative through our openness to the Divine Presence. Creativity deepens because we act in the dimension of grace. The transcendent life does not paralyze; it brings to birth; it inspires and guides creativity; it does not crush it.

Mid-life transcendence implies giving up one form of functionality in order to allow greater play to another form in service of the Kingdom. If functionality assumes the pose of being an end in itself, it becomes not only tyrannical in its demands but muffles spontaneity.

Creativity is a characteristic expression of the fact that the human being is called to live in the form or image of God, the Creator. We are co-creators with Christ. At the height of our functional life we may have performed for the sake of performance. The turn to transcendence is an invitation to break out of the chains we have forged for ourselves, to relinquish the thought of functional efficiency as an ideal in its own right, to restore creativity as a playful participation in divine powers transforming this world into the House of God.

The mid-life crisis is an opportunity to lose our life only to find it again in the creative Christ. To live creatively we need discipline. Otherwise outside forces usurp time and energy from our inner lives. Television, newspapers, movies — a disciplined enjoyment of them can be liberating, but enslavement can rob us of the benefits the middle years bestow. If there is any area where moderation, penance and mortification is necessary, it is here. The mid-life crisis can initiate a creative era or one of decadence. Do we refuse or grasp the hand God extends to us creatively?

The middle years call for our conscious decision to use and develop our creative potential. At the core of creativity is discipline and penance. For instance, to be free to create our own style of physical exercise in advancing age, we must first make a disciplined effort to learn about various exercises and try them out. Only then can we create a style of exercise that ties in with our personality and life situation. Discipline is needed to be faithful to these exercises and to keep adapting them to the needs that change with advancing years and physical ailments. Growing older, we must continually resist being reduced to dull routine. From time to time we should change our clothes or makeup, rearrange or renew our furniture, meet new people, read books, try a new restaurant or holiday resort, see a play or movie, take up a hobby, go on an adventurous trip, or enroll in courses that introduce us to new ideas. Through the asceticism of change in spite of growing inertia, we keep our incarnational abilities alert and alive; we remain a bridge for God's creative presence in this changing world.

Trust in the Transcendent increases our ability to take risks, to leap into the unknown, to put our past rigidities on the line, even at the risk of ridicule. With Christ at our side, no longer immersed in the mainstream of social life, we dare to try out lonely, untrod paths. No longer victims of the assembly line of our consumer society, we feel free to set aside time just to think, letting our mind and heart roam freely.

When the functional life dominated, we tended to use our mind mainly for critical appraisal. After the mid-life crisis we should allow ideas to come up freely and only assess and evaluate them at a later date. We should develop an interest in some form of art. It can be literature, movies, dance, painting, weaving, embroidery, calligraphy, pottery, music, the theater — whatever media of art can keep our creative powers alive. Creative openness may mean a shift of scenery and sources of interest in the years that find us freed from many social duties and distractions. Art may tie in with our newly developing transcendent perception, our religious experiences; it grants us a fresh outlook on ourselves and others and on the world around us as the House of God.

To foster transcendent creativity, we should not worry how others feel about our interests or expressions. The essence of such creativity is looking at the Divine Presence in all creation. If we are preoccupied with thoughts of acceptance, admiration, or remuneration, true transcendence is lost; we are dominated again by the vital and functional dimensions of the spiritual life. We have lost our wholeness. The reward of transcendent presence resides in itself, namely, in finding oneself in the mystery of the Divine. Creativity mirrors His image in limited forms of human originality and beauty.

Chapter XIII

THE MIDDLE YEARS AND
PRINCIPLES OF SPIRITUAL FORMATION

Spiritual formation starts out from two essential characteristics of human life. The first one is "form-ability"; it refers to the typical human ability in some measure to give form to one's life.

The second corresponding characteristic is the human dynamic of ongoing formation. The human person is always trying, at least implicitly, to give form to his life. In this book, we've looked for indications of this process in certain persons in mid-life: any attempt they might show, no matter how awkward and minimal, to give form to their unfolding in the middle years. We asked ourselves how they could deepen the spiritual formation mid-life asks of them. Briefly, we tried to respond to the questions that emerged from both the "form-ability" and the "ongoing formation process" we observe in certain people in the middle years of life.

We may call this spiritual formation process holistic, for it tends to give a unifying form to our life as a whole.

At times one or the other aspect of human formation may occasion a period of special development. We saw, for example, that functional skillfullness in social and professional life peaked for certain people in the first half of the middle years between 30 and 44. The mid-life crisis, however, occasioned in a number of those who were ready for it and had not yet passed through it, a special development of the transcendent dimension of life. Ultimately, however, these two developments would tend to come together in the unity of a well integrated holistic form of life.

Spiritual formation as holistic means that it tends to reintegrate various special developments within a harmonious spiritual style of life. During the mid-life crisis itself — as in other formation crises — it is more difficult to find this integration. The holistic tendency of spiritual formation is temporarily halted by the painful experiences of detachment from a former style of life and the hesitant initiation into a period of obscurity in which transcendence begins to announce itself. Only when we are at home with the transcendent dimension of our life will it be possible for the functional dimension of the former period to find its rightful place within the unique spiritual life form each of us is called to disclose in his or her life time.

Spontaneous Unfolding and Formation

At certain moments of life people feel compelled to think about what happens to them in their unfolding. What makes them stop and think is usually some problem that interrupts the spontaneous flow of self-emergence. A crisis disturbs their daily routine.

Where do such problems come from? Often they result from a tension inherent in development itself. It is a tension between our spontaneous self-unfolding and the typical spiritual formation that has to guide that unfolding.

At times our life seems to emerge effortlessly; aspirations, experiences, ambitions, decisions, actions — all arise spontaneously. We sense that we are growing in the right direction; we feel in harmony; life flows easily; self-unfolding is not a problem for us.

At other moments we are not so sure about the direction our life is taking. We begin to question the formative meaning of the situations we face. What do our experiences, desires, ambitions, acts and decisions mean? We feel the need for reflection, appraisal, guidance. We no longer trust our spontaneous growth; we ask ourselves how we should give form to our emergent life: in short, we ask ourselves about formation.

It is not surprising that questions about formation arise in us. We rarely feel totally at ease with our spontaneous unfolding. Often we feel the need to appraise what is going on in our daily development. We want to take a stand toward what happens in us. We like to take stock.

It seems clear from the above reflections that human development implies two poles: spontaneous unfolding and formation. If either of these poles falls away, our growth may be hampered or falsified.

We saw both poles present in our description of the mid-life crisis. The pole of spontaneous unfolding prevailed in the beginning. Vitally and functionally we experienced a decline of power. We experienced also an obscure spontaneous tending toward another form of life. We may have been inclined to suppress this role of spontaneous unfolding, to deny our decline, to cover it up with excessive self-exertion. Maybe we tried to escape the tendency towards deeper meaning in a frantic quest for new occupations. Later we reflected about what we were doing. How could we give form to this spontaneous unfolding? Gradually the tension between formation and unfolding diminished. At the end of the mid-life crisis we may have found a new form of life that integrated both poles, and pointed to our final unique life form in Christ.

Human Formation

What makes human formation human? Animal life unfolds spontaneously in the right direction; it is programmed by instinct and drive. Animals do not give form to their unfolding like people do. Animals, for instance, do not have a mid-life crisis. Many humans do. Humans have to complement their spontaneous self-emergence by formation.

Formation gives direction to and creates harmony among our countless desires, interests, ambitions, aspirations, skills, insights, feelings and motivations. They cannot be directed and unified by instinct. We aspire to integrate them into one harmonious form of life. We feel the need to "get our act together." We are able to attain this unifying form of life because of a capacity to rise beyond these separate and incidental developments. This "going beyond" creates the distance from them that we need in order to discipline them and integrate them meaningfully in a consistent spiritual form of life. We call this human power the transcendent dimension of our selfhood.

The word "transcend" means "going beyond" or "going more deeply into." We have an innate need and ability to look beyond what we feel and desire, beyond the situations we find ourselves in, beyond the partial and temporal unfoldings of our life here and now. This ability to go beyond or to go more deeply into enables us to make our formation typically human, superior to the spontaneous unfolding process in animal life.

Spiritual formation depends on this transcendent dimension. As we have seen, it is not isolated from the cultural, vital and functional forms of life. In fact, the transcendent direction affects all other dimensions of formation; it influences them and is influenced in turn by them. Spiritual formation is based on this fact. The more it succeeds in bringing together all these dimensions, the more transcendent and holistic our formation becomes.

Our reflections on the mid-life transcendence crisis illustrated this holistic aspect of formation. We saw how this crisis can only be solved if the person is able to look beyond his immediate feelings, desires, ambitions, and relations with self, others and world. We described how one can rise above the detachments he is exposed to in that period, how something awakens the person to aspirations that go beyond his immediate needs.

Differentiation

When we look more closely at the spiritual formation of life, we become aware of two movements: differentiation and integration. They form a polarity.

The movement of differentiation is one of discovering formative directives in life because of new life experiences. Formation implies that we are present to God, self, people, events and things as manifested in our life situations and in the communities whose life we share. In the process of formation our presence to life becomes increasingly differentiated. For example, a person may be present to God in meditative or contemplative prayer; to art in transcendent wonder; to his business as a well functioning manager; to his vital well being as a good jogger, swimmer and dieter; to physical nature as a keen experimental scientist. The spiritual image or form we most deeply are is operative in all these modes of differentiated presence. This differentiation gives birth to new insights, which may, in turn give rise to directives pertaining to the way we should give form to our lives concretely and effectively.

For example, the middle years of certain people are marked by a special differentiation of interests and directives, partly determined by the vital and cultural situations typical of the first and second half of the middle years. We should wisely foster these differentiations, but they are only one side of the story of ongoing formation.

Integration

If formation meant only differentiation, our life would soon become disorganized and lose its centeredness. Therefore, another dimension of formation has to complement this one — namely, the movement of integration. Differentiation divides, integration unifies our life. When an adolescent falls in love for the first time, he may be so absorbed in this experience that he temporarily loses the integration of his life. He may neglect other areas of living. He lets his studies slide, loses sight of his peers, is less attentive to family and friends. He needs the movement of integration to restore him to whole-ness; it will enable him to regain those lost areas of living, to re-incorporate them in his changing presence to reality.

Another example would be that of a person who discovers a new field of study. He becomes so involved in this research that he fails temporarily to be attentive to his family. Spiritual formation does not mean to deny these interests, ambitions and aspirations, but to integrate them within the whole of his life in light of transcendent life directives.

Differentiation and integration are spontaneous movements of unfolding. They stir in us before we try to give form to them. Spiritual formation takes these spontaneous movements into account and directs them prudently.

Growth always implies an ongoing differentiation of perception, experience, insight, interest, motivation, skill and commitment. This differentiation may lead to a temporary loss of balance at moments when a person feels overly anxious or excited about a new experience or field of interest. Momentary imbalance does not matter as long as he allows room for the movement of integration. He fosters this movement via patient presence to these initially unconnected experiences. Then he will be able to give all forthcoming formative directives a meaningful place in the totality of his life.

Exemplifying the integrative movement of formation is the process initiated at the successful termination of the mid-life crisis. The "autumn of life" that follows will find many past differentiations of the self being gradually reconciled and integrated.

Tensions Evoked by
Polar Movement of Formation

Fearing the tensions that may result from the polarity of this movement, we are tempted to say: "I have reached a moment of peace in my life; please let me stop differentiating. Don't get me involved in new persons, ideals, problems, interests, directions. Such differentiation may disturb the form of life I have attained; it takes time and energy to integrate new concerns in my life. Please, don't distress me with change; don't expose me to another environment, to other ideas or people. Don't interrupt my routine.

Don't demand activities that will disturb my daily ways. Leave me alone."

This lament is understandable. We may momentarily lose peace of mind. It does take time to integrate into our lives a new person, happening, concern or interest. Integration may demand a restructuring of the life form we were at ease with for years. It is the price we pay for growth. The alternative is to become fixated in our routines. If our life is no longer differentiating, we may die as persons before dying physically. Yet if we are to differentiate and integrate our lives spiritually, we cannot leave this developmental task to spontaneous unfolding alone. We have to be guided by spiritual formation, at least implicitly.

Integration should never be seen as a frozen "thing-like" state. Neither does it mean putting our perceptions, ambitions and aspirations "in a deep freeze" after integrating them neatly into our life. Integration is never a finished state; it is always an ongoing movement. This movement can go on only as long as there is something to integrate. In other words, integration is possible only when our self keeps differentiating. The differentiating-integrating movements of formation depend on one another.

The mid-life crisis was an example of the tensions evoked by any new life situation. We fear at that turning point to give up routines mastered during the functional period of the middle years. And yet we begin to realize how necessary it is for further growth to differentiate our life in a more transcendent direction. We realize also that we have to appraise wisely how much change we should open ourselves to at any moment.

Hierarchical Principle of Spiritual Integration

So far our foundational formation theory has given us some insight into the relation between formation and spontaneous unfolding. It clarified also how formation is a movement of differentiation and integration. Our presence to life becomes differentiated in various modes of presence; these modes in turn have to be integrated into a unique harmonious form of life. This integration will be colored by our personality, culture, philosophy and religion.

A basically serious person looks differently at life than a playful, humorous character; the intellectual type perceives things from another viewpoint than a practical man or woman; the world appears in a different light to a person of cool disposition than to one who is hypersensitive. Our culture too influences our transcendent outlook. People raised in an Eastern culture are different in many ways from those educated in Western schools of thought. The deepest influence on our spiritual formation may come from religion. Christians believe that the Holy Spirit Himself permeates their human power of transcendence. All of these factors contribute to each person's slowly emerging transcendent life direction.

In the light of this unifying destiny, we discover that we cannot live all differentiating modes of presence at the same time and with the same intensity. We cannot simultaneously look at TV, read a book, meditate, study, enjoy intimacy, play baseball, do physical exercises, and sketch paintings. In short, one mode of being must be preferred to another according to the demands of our life situation. For example, at one time we may enjoy the warmth of family encounter and not worry about our work; at another time we should take care of our job and not be overly distracted by worries about family problems.

Integration presupposes, therefore, a certain order of preference. To put this another way: formation by integration implies that we develop a flexible hierarchy of modes of presence. On the one hand, this order of interests and involvements should be flexible enough to adapt itself to changing situations. On the other hand, our transcendent life direction develops a basic order of interests that will prevail any time the situation allows. According to this hierarchy, one mode will be central in our unfolding lives while other modes will be subordinated in some order to this primary one.

The central direction of ongoing life formation will influence in some measure the directions taken by other modes of presence less central for us. For example, if my primary mode of presence is family intimacy I may prefer a job that gives me more time with my wife and children; my interest in outdoor sports may be curtailed by my need to be at home. If, on the contrary, I experience a special calling to be a creative scientist, I may feel inclined to spend less time with my family, to forego certain time consuming entertainments, to be less actively involved in politics, to spend many hours in the laboratory, and so on. In other words, the central formative direction of our life will imply similar but not identical directives in other modes less central for us. The conclusion is that our central mode of presence founds the empirical life form that will be ours in a certain period of formation.

Our preferred mode of presence does not necessarily exclude such modes as friendship, social involvement, love of nature, appreciation of esthetic surroundings, art, delicious food and pleasant entertainment. They can all be fostered without our losing integration as long as they do not oppose our central commitment. They must, however, be modulated by this main mode of presence in such a way that they stay in harmony with our unique formative direction of that period of our life.

In Christian formation the paramount question is how do we find increasingly — through these passing periodical forms of life — our unique image or form of god in whose likeness we are created? How do we find that unique form or image in Christ by whom we are liberated? How does our hierarchy of modes of presence increasingly harmonize with the form or image God meant for each of us from the beginning?

This development is clearly illustrated in our reflections on the spirituality of the middle years. The mid-life crisis may entail restructuring our hierarchy of modes of presence. Since transcendent modes of presence begin to prevail over functional ones after the mid-life crisis, our lives should be formed around them.

Vitalistic View of Self-Unfolding and Formation

Experience and observation make it clear that there is a spontaneous movement of growth in every human being. Spiritual formation is a dialogue between our transcendent self-dimension as formative and our spontaneous self-unfolding. A merely vitalistic or biological view of human emergence would deny that creative tension. In this view anything that is new in our development is not due to formation. It is simply the result of an unfolding of something like a blueprint laid down in our biological organism.

Of course, this biological theory of unfolding would not deny that the environment of the child has something to do with his growing up. But in this view the environment is utilized by the organism only in accordance with its innate blueprint. The environment merely offers useful matter for the unfolding organism.

The foundational theory of spiritual formation holds that while the innate laws of the organism do have a basic influence on the unfolding of the person, they cannot totally explain human formation. If human formation were only a question of autonomous biological growth, it would be impossible to give any form to this growth from a cultural or religious perspective. The person certainly utilizes his environment in service of his organismic needs and perceptions. But the environment also contains values. These cultural-spiritual values too have a directive influence on the development of the person. In interaction with biological influences, they become formative of the person as a whole in his transcendent as well as vital abilities.

How did the biological theory of self-unfolding originate? It is deduced, among other things, from organic growth in plants. The growth of a plant can only be influenced accidentally. For example, by manipulating temperature, light, and humidity we can slow down or speed up a plant's growth. Such accidental influences cannot change essentially the basic form that plant will assume once the growth process has taken its course.

The foundational spiritual view of formation holds, by contrast, that we can help ourselves and others to find a unique form of life. This view maintains that such a form can only be attained in light of a transcendent outlook. This outlook goes beyond mere biological determinations. To be sure these determinations are always influential. We must take them into account. But the way in which we do so depends on the values we allow to form our lives spiritually.

If growth or unfolding were a biological process only, no formation would be possible. The only meaningful aid to growth would then be the establishment of favorable organic conditions. Such conditions would not change the form the human organism should assume. This form would already be predetermined within the organism itself. This kind of help would only be accidental and of minor importance. It would not have any formative impact on the process of biological unfolding; it would remain exterior to this process itself. In this case the only assistance one could offer the unfolding organism would be that of care, protection and sustenance of the growth process. There would be no room left for any formation in the spiritual sense described earlier.

As we have seen, the spirituality of the middle years initiates a formation that goes beyond the biological decline of the organism. Formation at this time is not merely the blind execution of a blueprint laid down in a declining organism. Biological changes may trigger the mid-life crisis but the crisis cannot be reduced to them. The middle-aged person has to wait with patience for a sign of new transcendence in his life. Once that sign appears it should be tenderly cared for like a little flower that opens up between winter and spring. This sign, however weak, will tell us where to begin the task of transcendent transformation, which is the main task of the last half of life.

Chapter XIV

THE TRANSCENDENT SELF:
FORMATIVE DEATH AND RESURRECTION

The experience lived through by certain people in mid-life invites all of us to pay attention to our personal formation and its crises. The main themes of mid-life formation can be seen as symbols of the changes, conflicts, and crises of our spiritual growth at any time of life. One basic symbolic meaning underlies the process of mid-life transcendence: the recurring death and resurrection of the human life form. This need for dying recurs again and again in the history of our spiritual formation. Not every death leads to resurrection, for there are ways of dying that do not renew but impede further growth.

At certain moments of life I am faced with a crisis I can solve only by dying to the domination of a current form. I have no choice: I must decide either to die authentically to my past or to die inauthentically in a fixation on a past form that will make me stagnate. The spiritual death wish — permeated by the desire for resurrection — is crucial. It expresses the transcendent quality of all human unfolding and formation.

As human self, I am both "potentiality" and "actualization"; these are the two poles between which my spiritual life unfolds. Human potentiality is not something inert. On the contrary, my potentiality for growth is a dynamic tendency towards transcendence, which permeates all spiritual strivings. As soon as a new human potentiality announces itself in my life, I experience an inclination to realize it. For example, if my association with others has been on a merely pragmatic level, I may feel an aspiration to die to the exclusive domination of my functional approach to others and to become a more generous person. Until now, my world has been structured around the goal of utilitarian values only. This other possibility of a more transcendent way of life may change this one-sided approach. I can expect to experience a conflict between the old familiar way of functioning and the invitation to develop a generous form of presence to people, which will radically change my approach to them.

Crises of transcendence are often created by formative encounters with inspiring people whom I meet in person or in their writings. Such graced events expose me to the challenge of transcendence. When I affirm and actualize such a transcendent possibility, my world restructures itself around these new values.

Spiritual life, therefore, cannot be regarded as an object completed. I am "becoming"; I am potentiality for dying to my current form of life at any moment and rising to a form I am not yet. The human person is not closed in upon himself like a stone. We are a restless, spontaneous movement towards transcendence. We experience ourselves as incomplete, unfinished, longing to be. In short, the fact that I am a human being implies that I am called to repeated resurrection.

Every time I advance to a new mode of transcendence I am transformed. For example, I may be "born" to leadership after "dying" to overdependency on others. Leadership now becomes an aspect of my current form of life. This form carries with it new possibilities for death and resurrection. I may become a leader in a variety of ways formerly closed to me, for instance, administrative. Now leadership in administration becomes part of my current form of life. After some years I may experience the aspiration to expand beyond administrative to spiritual leadership. This new mode of leadership implies "death" to exclusive concentration on administrative achievements. Once again I may experience a crisis of transcendence confronting me with a choice. Even when I am partially formed by resurrection to a new form of life, I am never totally and finally formed. I always remain able to die and to experience a resurrection within the limits imposed on me by earlier life formations.

Whether I am a child or an adult, a simple person or a hero, a prisoner or a free citizen, I am always a potentiality for transcendence in many ways. If I were to "freeze" myself into one mold by repression of the aspiration to transcend what I currently am, I would die to authentic living. The most sordid crime against our humanity is to destroy what we basically are: transcendent selves.

We feel this innermost movement of life symbolized in nature itself. The setting of the sun at evening and its morning rising, the colorful death of nature in the fall and its resurrection in spring, have profound emotional significance. Centuries of cumulative literary and artistic tradition have intensified these symbols for us. They have been used to celebrate the death and resurrection of the spiritual form we give to our spontaneous unfolding. Even prehistoric people expressed this formative movement of transcendence in rituals symbolizing the renewal of the life of the tribe under the divine influence of the sun.

The process of spiritual death and resurrection takes place in various phases. The aspiration for a more transcendent life announces itself, first of all, as a dissatisfaction with past formation. Meanwhile, a restless anticipation of a new form of life springs up within me. Such formative discontent may invade me over and over again during my life, for my fullness is at the same time emptiness; my satisfaction is clouded by displeasure; my security is encumbered by uncertainty. No matter what success I experience, my contentment is never final; I carry with me always a secret desire to die to the old form of life and rise to the new. Paradoxically, my spiritual death wish itself will never die, for no form of life can ever fulfill me completely. Whether I form myself as organizer, leader, craftsman, thinker, artist, scientist or lover, I am never complete; I am always on the frontier of dissatisfaction with my past. Thus my "yes" to any current life form should never be ultimate.

The need to negate a current form of life in order to transcend beyond it may lead to self-depreciation. I could become bitter, bored or rebellious. Perhaps I aspire after new forms of life without knowing which ones I should be reborn to. Negation of a current form of life could also give rise to a self-destructive hatred of myself and my world. Only when death to a current form of life has been accomplished, and a period of mourning has purified and liberated me, will resurrection happen. I may then accept the residues of past forms in light of the present one. Instead of totally rejecting all past forms of life I can now, in a relativizing way, affirm the good residues left behind. I realize that these past forms of spiritual living were not worthless, but relatively valuable in light of this more transcendent form of presence. I can thus integrate past and present forms of spiritual living insofar as they all point to the unique image of the Divine I am called to from eternity. In this way I safeguard the continuation of my formation.

Formative death and transcendence is thus a dynamic process. First of all, the outward flow of life becomes stagnant. Enthusiasm is gone: I feel bored, disinterested, frustrated, not at home any longer in familiar routines. Gradually, the outward movement of my life is replaced by an inward movement, by recollection and self-presence. In recollection I become aware of possible forms my life could take on.

Emotional distance enables me to see life in a different perspective. This vision is the condition for transcendence. In meditating on my own potentialities and aspirations, my energies gather strength for resurrection.

This period of death and withdrawal is in effect a preparation for deeper life. I am suspended between the two poles of return to my former life form and progress to a wider, transcendent life orientation. Formative renewal is thus a spiritual sequence of frustration, withdrawal, new life orientation, and finally resurrection to a wider, transcendent form of life. If I did not die repeatedly, I should become encapsulated in past forms of life I have already realized.

Spiritual formation is marked by the crises all experience to a greater or lesser degree. They may be sudden or gradual, depending on the temperament and life history of the person involved. Whether the experience is cataclysmic or slow-moving, there is always a critical period in which the ultimate decision to hold back or go forward must be made. Every important decision of life implies a birth trauma of cutting myself free from a past in which I felt safely embedded like a foetus in the womb. Resurrection to a new life form means exposure to the threats of the unknown. This separation from the past is not passive. I must severe myself by a decision to accept a different, as yet untested, form of life as a daring thrust into the future. I must take the risk.

Moments of crisis often emerge when the meaning

of a particular form of life has collapsed. I experience that I must retreat and discover a different direction; I must make way for a new dimension of the spiritual life. The crisis is often evoked by the demand for commitment, whether in love or work, and from it is born personal responsibility.

The crisis is accompanied by stress: I am invited to risk the unknown yet feel inclined to cling to the safety of the past. If I risk the unknown I may or may not discover the stability and serenity I seek. Yet terrified by the uncertainty of the life ahead, fearful of the collapse of my current form, I hold fast to the old pattern. I suffer defeat because I will not risk the process of death and resurrection. At best, my refusal of renewal can result only in compromise. At worst, I will be burdened by constant spiritual guilt, for the invitation to transcendence can be repressed but not obliterated. I cling to false security rather than risk transcendence.

A formative life crisis occurs as a conflict between two poles or centers of energy in our personality. Each pole seems to give rise to its own perceptions, desires, and purposes. It is a dialectic of opposites, a living polarity between freedom and determination, potency and actualization, emptiness and fulfillment. I am stretched out between what I am and what I aspire to be. The formative crisis emerges when a demanding life situation actualizes this latent polarity, rooted as it is in the very structure of ongoing human formation.

In transcendent self-presence I become aware of

what life demands of me. Precisely at this crucial point, I can either freely surrender or hold on to my past. Humility and renunciation are necessary for effective resolution of the formation crisis. While I may perceive clearly the current form of life I should abandon, I cannot be certain about the opposite pole of this conflict — the deeper form of life calling to me as a vague ideal shrouded by the unknown.

The commitment which resolves the crisis is not so much a stern willfulness as a gentle yielding to new life with its subtle revelation of inspiration for the future. Self-surrender is the turning point in the process of death and resurrection, the either/or of my formative decision.

The fundamental polarity of human life between what is and what ought to be, between lack and fulfillment, between determination and freedom, is not abnormal; it is the norm. Every person is exposed to it because of the inescapable structure of human formation

We may conclude that formative crises have three phases: death, decision, resurrection. The death phase is one of frustration, anxiety, conflict. The phase of decision binds death to resurrection in the turning point of choice which implies transition to deeper living. The final phase of resurrection is one of transcendence, transformation and reintegration. These three aspects are so intertwined that it is often difficult to perceive them as distinct in the actual life situation.

The spiritual formation of every person involves a

chain of turning points. At each one of them, we are faced with the meaning of our current life form and called upon to decide. At such moments a recollection of myself in unifying inwardness is necessary; I must distance myself from a daily life of chaotic multiplicity. Even despair may be a gift which poses for me the choice between disintegration and integration of my life in light of the values I am called to commit myself to. I also become aware that I myself am destined always to move towards deeper integration. If I accept myself as essentially "form-able," as always in "ongoing formation," my life becomes a permanent possibility of new crises and decisions. Formation is thus not a performance to be achieved once and for all but a project to be courageously affirmed in every moment of choice.

The gift of transcendence is perhaps more to be prized in the contemporary world than ever before. I am in danger of losing spontaneity of life in the functionalized surroundings I am exposed to daily. An increasing number of institutional organizations may protect my life, but they also alienate me from my deepest aspirations. I need traditional systems to safeguard me, but I also need to revitalize and integrate them within my own divine calling. Finding my form of life implies a personalization of the wisdom of the past, a continual adaptation to both the old and new treasures of fundamental human experience illumined by grace and revelation. As a functional person, I find such formative assimilation and adaptation irritating and time-consuming.

To hurry things up, I categorize living traditions in streamlined systems and slogans. I begin to live by them as if they were inspiring life directives. Lacking a living dialogue with the wisdom of the past, my life becomes fragmented and alienated. I internalize the systems and slogans in the form of a superego which supplants my transcendent self. Empty structure replaces aspiration and inspiration.

To escape the benumbing systems that silence my aspirations, I must sacrifice functional security as ultimate and risk the adventure of death and resurrection. Refusing to accept the invitation to transcendence, I become a meaningless cipher in a lifeless structure. Without transcendence, I may suffer annihilation in the sense that I am emptied of my essential human quality of *always ongoing formation.*

The worst product of pragmatism is the "manufactured person," efficient but cold, devoid of aspiration, easily seduced to brutality and violence.

The pragmatic pursuit of occupations illustrates the danger of functionality without aspiration. Work can humanize or dehumanize a person. I may become a tool, a commodity, an instrument of impersonal production. Resurrection to a deeper meaning of action does not change the task; it changes its formative meaning. Instead of being merely a means of production, it becomes also an opportunity for growth, for service of humanity. As a creative expression of my unity with the divine direction of world and history, it may be lived as a liturgy. By contrast, when economic gain is my exclusive concern, work alienates me. Only when I care also for its transcendent meaning, can it make me whole.

I may become aware of the possible deadness of my life when faced with situations for which system and routine provide no answer. Suffering introduces me to myself, to encounter with the transcendent meaning of reality, and to dialogue with the voices of persons who existed before me and went through similar crises in their lives.

Here is the old story, the recurrent ritual of death and resurrection. If I desire to live and grow, I must suffer; I must renew the formative thrust of my life in an act of sacrifice. I may have to renounce primitive impulses, status seeking, and egocentrism, but such an offering symbolizes my willingness to renounce a fixated past identity as a condition for rising anew as a more transcendent self.

Chapter XV

FORMATIVE TRANSCENDENCE: NEGATIVE PHASE

The terms "crisis of transcendence" or "spiritual formation crisis" do not refer to the ordinary crises of daily life. They apply to significant formation situations involving a redirection of one's current life form. Such redirection is meant to attune a person more finely towards the graced form he or she is called to live uniquely. The spiritual formation crisis that both renews and deepens transcendence involves in turn death and resurrection. The death experience is the negative stage of the crisis of transcendence. If one becomes fixated in this phase, he may be unable to experience the resurrection which normally follows the working through of the death experience.

In some people a transcendence crisis may be initiated by personal tragedy. Faced with loss of dear ones, job, health, status or possessions, they may respond with hope or despondency. Despondency is difficult to overcome as long as one cannot affirm the possibility of transcendence in seemingly intolerable situations. Hope, by contrast, affirms self-formation in face of the odds of life. On the frontier of the tolerable, it says yes to the divine power that forms our lives mysteriously. People who do not grow to this trust may regard such situations as absurd. They refuse the adventure of ongoing formation, sadly to their own detriment. In a few persons the negative stage manifests itself more dramatically in a revulsion against past forms of life; it may lead to despair, suicidal tendencies, or self-destruction through alcohol or drugs.

Most people drift into a crisis of transcendence without being aware of the source of their discomfort. Others who flow with the formative powers in and around them gain insight into their predicament. Gradually they begin to understand the formative meaning of these negative feelings. With this growing comprehension, new outlooks for future living emerge. Their response to such prospects determines the subsequent direction of their life.

Some people evade the transcendence crisis altogether. They lack the courage to face the challenge of formation, to choose either trust or distrust, hope or despondency, resistance or surrender. They prefer false security to a confrontation with the sacred powers that challenge human life. Sooner or later they are prone to an all-pervading "formation guilt" — the source of which they cannot pinpoint. This kind of guilt follows the refusal of the invitation to transcendence. Ordinarily this guilt feeling is repressed; it manifests itself in a variety of spiritual, psychic and somatic symptoms. Clearly, their rejection of humanity-as-ongoing-formation demands its price.

Though the negative phase of a formation crisis has certain common characteristics, the experience of it varies with each person. People suffering in it may go through a "dark night" preliminary to decision and transcendence; they may be overwhelmed by distrust and despair or by negativism, anger, cynicism, and self-depreciation.

Ordinarily the formative phases of death, decision and resurrection are so interlocked that they resist neat delineation. The negative stage implies a disintegration of one's current life form. This process is punctured by moments of insight and by partial decisions made in light of newly disclosed options. It is difficult at any stage of this development to point out precisely the beginning of a crisis of transcendence or the crucial moment of decision beyond which there is no return.

Some people who face the crisis may delay its solution by opting for a different, but as yet congenial form of life. Gradually they may become aware of their mistake; transcendent self-reflection helps them to see the inauthentic inclinations that led to self-deception. A period of purifying repentance follows. The search for a congenial life form is resumed. Finally, after much trial and error and many partial decisions, the search ceases: a congenial life form is disclosed and accepted. Again, it is difficult to pinpoint exactly the moment at which the uncongenial option is overcome; at which repentance has achieved its purification; at which the right form is initiated. In retrospect the whole process in all its phases points to the mystery of redemption from a less authentic form of life to one more in tune with the unique divine form or image I am called to by the Lord.

Though the stages of each one's struggle are not clearly demarcated, the negative phase of the transcendence crisis always begins with a dissatisfaction over one's present form of life. The crisis may be precipitated by a gradual or sudden awareness that the way I am present to reality has become counterproductive. The solution of the crisis will be postponed as long as I negate the always ongoing demand for creative self-formation.

In formative spirituality the term "negation of formation" has a specific meaning. Obviously, it is not about formation in a functional, vital, or social sense, such as formation of the muscles and other faculties of the body or formation of technical, intellectual, manual and social skills. Formation means here spiritual or holistic formation. It refers to cooperation with the mystery of the powers of spiritual formation that grace each person's life. I commit myself to the divine form I am uniquely called to live in dialogue with the possibilities and limits disclosed to me over a lifetime.

To be in tune with the powers of spiritual formation means to be lifted beyond the merely functional and, at the same time, to be inspired to functional involvement in the world. For example, a person may be called to a periodic life form that implies more extensive social involvement; inspired by this call, he may decide to incarnate his concern functionally in such activities as slum clearance, anti-poverty projects, or civil rights movements.

In any harmonious form of life, we note a consonance between faithfulness to one's life direction and to its incarnation in functional projects. Indeed, much of the perennial appeal of the saints lies in the consistency between their aspirations and daily deeds of valor. Saints are extraordinary versions of the persons many of us would like to be. Compare how disappointed we feel when we sense discrepancy between someone's life and aspiration, when we see, for instance, vulgarity of word and action in a sensitive woman.

The human person is capable of splitting off his practical pursuits from his openness to the divine direction. He may build a career impressive to people while he himself becomes estranged from his deepest call. Life thus impoverished can become pompous, boring, of no transcendent purpose. This person's preoccupation with pragmatic projects is heightened by the intoxicating acclaim of those who admire his performance. It becomes more and more difficult for him to admit to his emptiness; an abyss of loneliness looms up. Threatened by this abyss, the merely functional person runs away from insight into his real situation. He represses awareness of the wasteland inside. Response to the mystery of his life direction becomes increasingly negative. Indeed he *must* negate his transcendent call more and more. Any acknowledgement of lack of depth threatens his repression. If his defenses against the transcendent self were to break down, he would have to face the nothingness in which he lingers. His life may degenerate into a frantic pursuit of defensive distractions.

It is impossible to make surface activity and its shallow gain one's final goal. Therefore, the wholly functional person must make *himself* the ultimate purpose of life. The love that ought to embrace the mystery that grounds his life reverts exclusively to himself as isolated from his ground. He gropes for meaning in life by grasping for power, status, and possession. Instead of meeting others respectfully in their unique self-emergence, he manipulates them to serve his projects. His pretense of passion hides his impotence for love. His conquests are mere assays at pleasure and dominance; they touch only the surface of the other while love would fathom his mystery.

Anyone who leads such a life may die without being aware that he did not allow his unique form to emerge. Others are impelled by a traumatic experience or flash of insight to face their failure. As we have seen, in many people in our culture such a crisis may not erupt before middle age. It is at once a blow and a gift. It shocks one into acknowledgment of the vacuum life has become. A first result of this discovery is a loss of satisfaction; one's activity now seems devoid of meaning. The clamor of admirers sounds hollow. Erotic adventures no longer fulfill one's longing. He suffers a let-down that paralyzes impulses and ambitions. Bored by his past, he feels burnt-out in the present.

This kind of negative experience tends to reverse one's love-hate relationships. If a person formerly idolizes his life, he is now inclined to demonize himself. A similar reversal happens in relation to others. Before the crisis he may have idolized successful others, ignoring their limits and deficiencies. Now in the phase of demonizing, pained by disappointment, he may detest those he previously idolized.

Both forms of totalizing are unrealistic. They do not see life as it is, as a limited but true manifestation of the formative goodness, truth, and beauty of the divine presence in this world. A person in a negative stage perceives only the defects of those who fail his previous adulations. He loses temporarily his awareness of the limited or at least potential goodness present in every human being. His style of life does not yet comprehend the tempered wisdom and mellow judgment of a mind that has transcended both deifying and demonizing.

John Steinbeck's novella, *The Pearl,* tells the story of a Mexican fisherman, Kino, who one day dives into the sea and finds an oyster that contains a priceless pearl. Kino immediately divinizes his possession. He directs all his hopes for a full and happy life to his precious jewel. When he discovers that his pearl brings him only anguish and despair, he demonizes his former treasure and casts it back into the sea.

Kino symbolizes all of us who, in the crisis of transcendence, demonize what we once deified.

An excessively negative crisis may lead to a boredom so pervasive that the person feels himself sinking into blank despair. He has come to the end of everything that gave meaning to his life. He is tasting to the full its emptiness. He is so wounded that he cannot bear any lightheartedness in others. To him they are lost in the superficialities of life. He pities them for not sensing the triviality of all that seems so important to the average person.

Undoubtedly, the number of "burnt-out cases" is bound to increase in a society that prepares people for pragmatic lives. Contemporary culture tends to be one-dimensional. Its formative effort concentrates on the functional development of life with a subsequent neglect of the transcendent mode of presence. As a result, many contemporaries, particularly those in the second half of life, become victims of mere functionality. They live out their last years in quiet desperation. A number despair and destroy themselves through direct or indirect suicide; others achieve a solution of their crisis by working it through in their own way. Many live or die in a wasteland of despair that reflects the contemporary situation.

The condemnatory responses typical of a person in this crisis cannot be accepted as objectively valid. They are vivid expressions of the emptiness he endures. When the meaningfulness of existence is no longer experienced, life loses its lustre. It is as if the central lighting system of a city is struck by a tornado and all the lights go out. When the system recovers its power, the lamps flare on; they radiate their limited, but needed brilliance. They break through the darkness of the city like innumerable stars.

Something similar happens when a transcendence crisis is worked through successfully. The life of the person gains depth and meaning. In light of this meaning, he is able to see the relative significance and beauty of himself and others, of events and things. They light up again, dispelling the fearful darkness of his perception during the negative phase of the crisis.

One possible accompaniment to negativity is an ironic attitude toward life. Irony as a mode of formation may be good or bad, helpful or harmful, fostering of growth or inhibiting it. Depending on the formation situation, any of these opposites may be true. The ironical approach to reality may be beneficial as a temporary means of relativizing persons, things or institutions overvalued in the past. Irony may be used to destroy the false gods in one's life so that the true God may appear. Irony can also function as a sharp instrument to pierce the veil of pretense shrouding unwelcome truth. As formative, it is a means of de-masking reality, of seeing through the false pretensions of people, things, and institutions.

Irony can perform a formative function for society as a whole, and particularly for the well balanced individual. But the victim of a negative transcendence crisis is often too deeply wounded to benefit from irony that others direct against him. He can only bear irony about himself when it emerges from within. It can be a blessing if it is only passing and does not deteriorate into cynicism.

In the negative phase of the transcendence crisis, irony may have a special meaning. It may help the person undo the deification of his past and free him to uncover true values. Still the danger is present that the person may become fixated in his ironic approach. In that case, all other modes of formation become centered around an ironic life form. Outlook and behavior become permanently negative. No possibility appears for the breakthrough of a joyous approach to self-formation. The ironic person may have learned to transcend the pretenses of life, but he has not yet grown to its daily celebration in light of his formative call.

In certain people irony may manifest itself throughout the negative phase of a transcendence crisis. At the end of this stage, as the moment of resolution approaches, a new understanding of life announces itself. Irony has prepared the way for the perception of one's true life form by devaluing that which is counterfeit. It has unmasked the pretenses that concealed from the person the humble truth of his calling. The negative crisis has made him aware of what his real call is *not*. In this disclosure of what his calling is *not*, there appears a first glimpse of what it might be. In this sense the ironic mode of life may manifest indirectly — as through a glass darkly — a more transcendent meaning of life. Obscurity thus marks the beginning of the struggle for transcendence and irony is often its expression.

The real solution of the crisis of transcendence implies the dissolution of irony. Humor takes its place as a sign of deliverance from the negative phase. A relaxed atmosphere pervades the self, erasing the traces of aggressive irony.

To grow in transcendent presence is to grow in humor. Transcendence implies the experience of contrast between the things of time and the things of eternity. An incident once blown out of proportion now evokes a patient smile. When the vital and functional dimensions of the spiritual life prevail, we tend to magnify molehills into mountains. We allow our irrational, romantic selves to be seduced by cultural fads. We resemble schoolgirls looking in a department store window and squealing with rapture over some trinket displayed under glaring lights. Passersby smile at the ecstatic effect produced by so small an item.

People still dominated by the romantic and functional dimensions of the spiritual life seem bound to such enticements. Since they are legion in our culture, the transcendent person often meets with situations that make him smile inwardly in good humor and kind understanding. He laughs at himself too. Humility and peace of mind free him from ego-idealization and its defenses. He is able to accept in good faith his own deficiencies. His lighthearted remarks are crystallizations of a loving, humorous vision of reality. They mark him as a person who measures romantic and functional values against the horizon of transcendent norms.

Transcendent humor does not emerge at once. In some its birth must be preceded by the ironic attitude of the negative phase of transcendence. Irony lacks the mellowness, compassion, joy and light-heartedness of transcendent humor; it clings to the negative side of things. In the ironic phase, one is often unable to sympathize with human weakness. He cannot yet appreciate that this fallen world, with all its miseries, is still the beloved House of God in whose providence all things will end well ultimately.

* * * *

Real encounter with affirmative others is another aid to transcendence. Genuine love implies some opening up to the Infinite, a going beyond the changing appearances of everyday life. Love and friendship can play an important role in a crisis of formation. For many life may remain meaningless as long as they do not discover the mystery of infinite care in encounter with caring others. The frustration and futility of life in the negative stage may be compared to a starless night. Some are caught in this darkness permanently. Their life deteriorates into a pattern of disappointment and bitterness. The power for growth is paralyzed; nothing has meaning. Others move toward the slow dawn of self-recognition; they pursue a hesitant passage through the maze of self-deception towards final acceptance of their life call, often in encounter with a "soul friend" who really cares.

Love can be a powerful aid when a person begins the long journey out of the darkness of the negative phase. His first glimpse of life occurs often in encounter with affirmative others. As he begins to doubt himself, to become aware of the irony of his idolization of self or others, he is ready to see himself and them in a clearer light. His painful awareness of emptiness and failure still implies a certain self-absorption. This makes it difficult to encounter others in their uniqueness. He sees them not in themselves, but in relation to his own growing self-awareness. His perception differs, however, from that of the past. In the face of insecurity he could only feel at home with others to the degree that they enhanced his imagined importance. Now he can accept them also as reminders of his deficiencies. Encounter with them enables him to face both false and true aspects of his self-image.

The grace of true encounter offers not only an opportunity for deeper self-understanding but also the encouragement of affirmation, respect, and understanding in spite of the ugly outbursts this crisis may give rise to. If the person is fortunate enough to find such generosity in a fellow human being, he will be helped considerably along the way. This encounter will foster the disclosure of his true life form which, until now, may have been weakly developed, covered over by layers of self-exalting fantasies, rigid defenses, and repressed feelings of guilt due to his betrayal of the life call.

Encased in his counterfeit form, he was unable to follow the divine call as it revealed itself in his life situation. Instead, he substituted the approval of crowd or collectivity for the divine affirmation itself. It became crucial for him to appear attractive or powerful in the eyes of people. While he may have been a "hit" according to vulgar standards of success, he was a misfit in the realm of transcendent values. Then he received the grace to distance himself, perhaps through ironic relativization, from the counterfeit values that made him overdependent on inauthentic pulsations in his culture. Now he finds the grace of encountering a formative person, who will accept him unconditionally when he reveals his deficient self in all its failure and fragility.

In affirmative encounter, the person may dare to open up to his true self for the first time — no matter how feeble and crippled this emergent self may be. This openness enables him to find his way in light of the mysterious call echoed through the veil of every-dayness. This newly gained freedom does not exclude the possibility of erratic options at odds with his call.

Anyone can err temporarily in his choices. What is important at this end point of the negative crisis is that the option is actually his own. Openness implies acknowledgment also of the consequences of uncongenial options. He discerns their undesirability through their deformative effects. With such appraisal, he may experience repentance and resolve to try again. He realizes that he has missed or betrayed his unique direction. In this way he accepts responsibility for his life. He becomes accountable. Responsibility means here an enlightenment and enlargement of the heart. It means the ability to respond wisely and wholeheartedly to what reveals itself in the daily situation as one's direction. Before this transcendence crisis, the person was less able to respond this way. The divine summons of every-dayness was still veiled by his narcissism. His life was not sufficiently "counter cultural" to obey the whisper of the spirit.

A person who idolizes himself, his culture or community, cannot experience the re-generation characteristic of true repentance. Deification of self or community leads to the illusion of creating either alone or with others one's life direction rather than responding to God's inspiration, which is a gift, not a self-initiated product. If a person or community attempts to produce their own way of life, they become their own standard of formation. They feel as if they do not need to repent of their mistreatment of self, nature, and others, for these are mere objects in a world of their own making.

Openness to the mystery of God's presence in all that is makes us sensitive to the consequences of our controlling approaches. It gives rise to repentance and responsibility. These are sources of true formation. By gradually expanding his openness, the person is released from the burnt out form of life he once totalized. He accepts at last that he has to grow to a way of life he experiences increasingly as gift. From now on, he may experience formation not as a product he invents but as a mystery he must live in openness and love.

Our life on earth is a slow process of ongoing formation, of increasing transcendence through passing life forms of greater or lesser darkness. The light seen dimly in each higher form of one's divine likeness is a source of joy and dynamism. It is the light of God's image in the center of each person's being that begins to illumine all dimensions of his life.

Chapter XVI

FORMATIVE TRANSCENDENCE: POSITIVE PHASE

When despair seems invincible and life itself absurd, we may experience paradoxically the beginnings of the positive phase of a transcendence crisis. We feel released for a short duration from emptiness and desolation. The recurrence and deepening of such moments depends on our option for life over death, for transcendence over stagnation.

The negative phase of the crisis can now be seen as a prelude to our release from a past form of life no longer in tune with the summons of the present. We dare to hope that life will be meaningful again. We move through anguished decision towards a new mode of self-formation. Anxiety rises as we feel called to an option that may alter our entire life. Our agonized self-expression reflects this inner conflict. Precipitated into the climax of a transcendence crisis, we are often overcome by hesitation. We feel the invitation to transformation as a threat to our very being. Life itself seems to disintegrate. In dialogue with divine intimations, we become aware of our current form as somehow inadequate; it is no longer a pointer to the unique form of life we are called to mysteriously.

The formative situation we face arouses us from slumber; it forces us to self-disclosure. The crisis creates a mood of detachment from our familiar world. Our former life directives are doubted; therefore, the world of meaning corresponding to them loses its stability. We experience self and world as strange, mysterious, incomplete.

At the peak of a transcendence crisis, we go beyond the commonplaces of our everyday world. We become aware of the limits of our current form of life. This awareness already connotes transcendence of these limits We heed the call to become the unique image of the Divine we most truly are. New life directives light up for us. The daily defenses that protect our current form of life begin to crumble. We suffer a sharp change from our ordinary pace. As the moment of personal decision approaches, we feel lonely. The peak of a transcendence crisis, which compels decision, not only isolates us temporarily from our former life; it places this life — with all its deceptions — before our eyes in sharp-edged contours. We are lifted, as it were, to a lonely plateau where we observe our life from a distance, like a mountain climber who looks down upon his village when the clouds have moved away. Our detached vision clears the cloudiness of concealment which makes it difficult to see who we are.

The transcendence crisis thus implies a disruption of our taken-for-granted world. It shows us the irrelevancy of many exaggerated concerns. We feel anxious in the face of this revelation. We sense that the crisis is not only crushing but elevating; we experience possibilities of formation unsuspected before.

Fascinated by the promise of liberation for a deeper life, we reach the turning point of decision. The crisis has freed us to realize new potentialities. We are now called to take the leap of transcendence to a higher form of life. If we decline the opportunity, we will feel guilty not only for what we omitted but for refusing to be who we are. We feel indicted by life itself, by the emergent divine image within us, inviting us to rise beyond our momentary form. It is as if we are brought to trial, forced to accept or reject the demands of the life call. We realize that we must make a response in conscience to what we are called to be.

Our answer is the turning point from one form of life to another more in tune with the unique divine image that will ultimately be revealed in us. For the Christian this positive option leads to a moment of rebirth or resurrection in Christ in whom one's own divine image is contained.

The person rising anew in Christ begins to live a form of life that approaches the mystery of the final divine image he is called to from eternity. This form is one step further in the disclosure of his divine identity. His transcending option fosters growth toward integration. He has unveiled a little more his hidden call, his divine destiny; he has affirmed his heritage, the divine image within, with all its inherent possibilities. He is freed from a multiplicity of fragmented incidents and isolated moments. He recalls the past and anticipates the future in light of this resurrection. He lives in a more committed style of presence to each moment of life integrated within this direction and is less and less dispersed in his self-formation.

This resurrection, he knows, is not his accomplishment; it is a gift that evokes in him awe and wonder. The mystery of divine formation transcends his own power and expectation. It cannot be compelled, only received. The resurrection at the end of the crisis is accompanied by feelings of joy, peace, and serenity. Having recovered his center in the Divine, he feels more and more confident. Such confidence differs from the complacency that may have marked his past. Before this recovery of the truth of who he is, he was often lulled into the false security of functional perfectionism. Now he sees this posture as a defense against disclosure of the divine image at the heart of his existence and a resistance of its invitation to surrender.

The self-presence of the transcendent person is the opposite of self-satisfaction; it implies increased presence to the divine form at the core of his being, which inspires yet surpasses his empirical self; it also evokes dissatisfaction because the form to be given to his empirical self does not yet flow harmoniously from the mystery within. Increased in-touchness with the unique image he is in God helps him to transcend the temptation to blind conformity.

The serenity experienced at the center does not take away anxiety; it enables one to live with it. The resurrection to a form of life more finely attuned to the divine form assures him that he is moving in the right direction for this period of his personal history. In unfolding this current form, he must follow directives emerging from the divine image within that gives rise to ever fresh inspirations. These directives are disclosed in dialogue with life situations in which the Spirit also speaks. They often imply that a person must tear himself away from the familiar in order to be faithful to the life form called forth in him. At such moments anxiety is unavoidable. He can only cope with it because of a deeper serenity at the root of his life where the divine image dominates.

After experiencing transcendence of a past life form that had lost its efficacy as a signpost on the journey, the person returns to his daily surroundings with a sense of reverence. He dialogues with his situation from a transcendent point of view. Having abandoned certain familiar directives, he reviews formative motivations in light of his changed vision. Resurrection often implies for him a transformation from certain viewpoints once shared with crowd or collectively to unique directives that flow from the divine form within. For example, in the universal treasures of sacred tradition, he is able to read also a personal message.

In this positive phase the person begins to realize that life is a recurrent sequence of death and resurrection. One moves with grace towards ever higher transcendence until the empirical form of life is in harmony with the divine image slumbering at the center of his being. Christ's death and resurrection is a prototype of the recurrent transcendence crisis we are called to pass through in our journey to the divine image hidden within.

The so-called mid-life crisis that people in certain cultures may experience at that time of life symbolizes any transcendence crisis we may undergo. Its meaning is the transition to a more advanced stage of formation. This transition happens through disclosure of the life call that issues from the divine image in the center of one's being.

Recurrent renewal by transcendence crises prevents the deterioration of life into a stereotyped pattern; it also revitalizes tradition as a source of formation. As noted above, we are called to give form to our empirical self in light of the unique divine image at the root of our being. This form must be achieved in a succession of life situations already structured by tradition. Such structures could paralyze my life. To prevent this from happening, I must revitalize the wisdom of tradition that is buried in these structures. The resurrection phase of the transcendence crisis can restore life to tradition and tradition to life. It implies the reinstitution of formative dialogue with the structures I meet in daily life. This dialogue infuses life into the skeleton of tradition. Transcendent formation thus occurs as a dialogue between tradition as given and my call to form an empirical self that is faithful to my divine image and to the justified demands of tradition, body, psyche, and world.

My aspiration for resurrection will never be fulfilled in this life. No transcendence crisis takes away totally my incompleteness and vulnerability. Human life always has about it an element of mediocrity. Recurrent rebirth saves me, however, from sheer mediocrity. While much mediocrity is part of the human predicament, sheer mediocrity would be incompatible with ongoing formation.

It would be wrong to ascribe alienation from my divine image only to my environment and not to myself. Like everyone else, I am in some measure commonplace, selfish, corrupted. The unavoidable need to comply with an already structured world can become an estranging force for all persons. The art of formation demands that I affirm my need for structure, and, at the same time, make frozen structures fluid again by my creative presence. When I do not accept this two-pronged challenge, I may either become the complacent victim of lifeless structures or rebel against my dependence on them in a violent attempt to leap over the limits of my formative powers. I try to burst the bounds of human reality and force a final resurrection, thus repudiating the necessity of gradual incarnation.

Human formation happens in phases. This means it is dependent on the limitations of successive phases of human development and on the concrete situations in which this development takes place. Denial of the gradualness of formation, rebellion against its limits, leads to deformation. Recognition of such deformation creates the insight that life itself is limited, that formation is bound to dialogue with developmental stages and situations. Willful formation depicts puny man beating his fists against a reality he cannot control, only to become aware in the end that he is a sorry creature trying to play God. Indeed one may be tempted after passage through a transcendence crisis to immoderation in further formation attempts. This temptation is due to the feelings of release and power we experience at the end of this crisis.

Excessive and lasting rebellion against tradition is another threat to wholesome formation. True formation implies the attempt to escape absorption in lifeless conformity. To drink from the springs of living tradition requires a gesture of separation from outworn customs and conventions, but I do run the risk of becoming fixated on this gesture of separation. If repudiation remains merely that, I may be condemned to a life of nihilism.

To be sure, it is necessary to separate myself inwardly from mere conformity to create room for the unique expression of my formation. This rebellion against the alienating potential of tradition may lead to the exalted vision of an autonomous formation that could surpass entirely the bounds of situation and incarnation. When this happens, I rebel against human nature itself. I aspire to that total freedom of formation that is the ultimate self-deception. I exchange one kind of alienation for a worse one — alienation from my limited divine image, from compassion with my companions on the journey, from the world, from life itself.

To opt for autonomy of formation is to choose a schizoid life, cut off from reality. On the one extreme, we may become "pious plodders," who compulsively act without attention to the flow of real life; on the other extreme, we may become "holy floaters," who have lost touch with everydayness. We may begin to perceive all law and authority as a threat to self-formation. Self-surrender in love becomes difficult when we fear any ties with others that might limit our freedom of formation.

To avoid this ultimate alienation, I must die not only to lifeless convention but also to the dream of autonomous formation. I must submit to the authority of the limited situation in which my ongoing formation has to incarnate itself.

When I have achieved the challenge of greater transcendence, I must not refuse the limited heroism my life form may demand. If I attempt to be absolutely heroic, which is arrogance, I shall feel guilty; if I fail to be heroic at any time, in any way, which is cowardice, I shall feel guilty too. Once I have accepted my call to live a life that is necessarily part heroism and part mediocrity, I must live out these two dimensions of my formation with some degree of serenity. We must accept both the heroism and the mediocrity all human formation implies since the Fall.

The positive transcendence crisis and its consequence of resurrection is, therefore, a call to heroism within human limits. It confronts the person with a paradoxical life of simultaneous nobility and mediocrity. It makes the person aware of what it means to rise through hardship to the stars: *per aspera ad astra.* From the dust of the earth, the human spirit reaches for the heavens. Such is the truth of our transcendent formation.